BARRON'S PARENTING KEYS

KEYS TO SUCCESSFUL STEP-FATHERING

Second Edition

Carl E. Pickhardt, Ph.D.

BARRON'S

Material in this book was gathered from my experience counseling with stepfamilies and conducting numerous parenting workshops over the years. All examples given and quotations used, however, are fictional, created to illustrate a psychological point.

Acknowledgments

I would like to thank my wife, Irene, for her help in the final stages of this manuscript, and the Barbara Bauer Literary Agency for continuing to represent my interests well and for providing me with a much needed dose of perspective as a writer.

All inquiries should be addressed to:
Barron's Educational Series, Inc.
250 Wireless Boulevard
Hauppauge, New York 11788
www.barronseduc.com

ISBN-13: 978-0-7641-4336-6
ISBN-10: 0-7641-4336-0

Library of Congress Control No. 2009048938

Library of Congress Cataloging-in-Publication Data
Pickhardt, Carl E., 1939-
  Keys to successful stepfathering / Carl E. Pickhardt.
    p. cm. — (Barron's parenting keys)
  Includes bibliographical references and index.
  ISBN-13: 978-0-7641-4336-6
  ISBN-10: 0-7641-4336-0
  1. Stepfathers. 2. Stepfamilies. I. Title.
  HQ756.P52 2010
    306.874'7—dc22

                                                    2009048938

PRINTED IN THE UNITED STATES OF AMERICA
9 8 7 6 5 4 3 2 1

DEDICATION

TO MY STEPFATHER, FRANK WILSON

I could not have written *Keys to Successful Stepfathering* without having had Frank, my stepfather, in my life. A brave man, he married a woman with three children, two already in adolescence. With marriage came his commitment to support this instant family, a responsibility about which I never heard him complain.

Back in the 1950s, there were no books or organizations around to guide reconstituted families through the minefield of steprelationships, but somehow Frank managed to find a way that worked. Looking back, it seems to me that he did a lot of things right. Of course he wasn't perfect, but then neither was I, and that was okay. Because he accepted and respected me as I was, I did the same with him.

In all my teenage years, I don't remember him ever criticizing me. What I do remember, however, is his occasionally questioning some of my choices and offering measured, clear advice. For example, although he understood my frustration with the endless classroom lectures, he suggested that I might want to delay my decision to drop out of college until I finished my freshman year. "Get the first year behind you and then decide what you want to do," he said. Because I followed his advice, I owe my college graduation in part to him.

A quiet, steady man of few words, Frank made little effort to parent me. And he made none to "father" me, because I already had a dad. By just being present he was an emotionally and financially stabilizing force to the entire family.

As an engineer, he was a professional problem solver, a role that was absolutely consistent with how he was away from work. For him, problems of any kind were simply part of life. They were nothing to get upset about. They were only to think about and fix as best one could. Then one moved on to the next, because that was just life—one problem after another. Although I will never be as patient and practical as Frank was, what patience and practicality I do have when confronting problems I believe I owe to him. I benefit from this "step-education" to this day.

CONTENTS

INTRODUCTION

When a mother remarries, a steprelationship is created between her children and her new husband. The purpose of this book is to describe some of the contributions a stepfather can make to remarried family life, some of the common pitfalls in his path, some of the constructive alternatives he can choose, and some of the satisfactions he can enjoy.

Coming from different living situations, past experiences, traditions, histories, and biological attachments, this man and these children are thrust into household intimacy and are expected to function together as a family unit. Harmoniously integrating all of these differences is an ongoing challenge of stepfamily life. The task is neither simple nor easy. First socially, and then psychologically, these new relationships can become extremely complex and confusing. *Stepfamilies mix people up.* At first, it is hard to figure out how to act and react, and how to fit in and how to get along.

As with *in-laws*, steprelatives can be people one does not know, understand, or necessarily like that well. Suddenly, strangers become linked together as *family*. Learning to live with step-ties takes time and patience. In-laws and steprelatives are both *appendage relationships*. They are created as a function of two people marrying or remarrying. In this process, the partners commit to some degree of consideration for each other's extended family. Part of their unstated vows usually includes an acceptance of this commitment: "For the sake of my union with you, I will try to have a good relationship with your parents, and with your children. I didn't marry you for them, but I married knowing they came attached to you, and you to them. Therefore, I will try to honor that attachment."

The similarity between in-laws and steprelationships ends, however, where the experience of daily living together and responsibility for daily caretaking begins. During their courtship, couples usually discuss what stepfamily life will be like. Filled with love for each other and hope for a happy future, they rely on how they all get along before marriage to predict how they will get along afterward. Role changes, however, change relationships. *Once the fun-loving friend of their mother moves in and begins acting like a serious second parent, the relationship changes for the stepchildren. Once the welcome children of his wife-to-be become a source of daily interference in his new marriage, the relationship changes for the stepfather.*

None of them bargained for this friction in their relationship. What's going wrong? Nothing. Reality is just setting in. They need to *not* take difficulties personally that are built into the dynamics of steprelationships—dynamics that are discussed throughout this book. They need to *not* feel guilty and to *not* blame each other for what is no one's fault. Confronting problems for which earlier experience has not prepared them, they all begin encountering some of the powerful tensions built into the fabric of stepfamily life. No matter how well managed, as long as they all live together, these tensions will never go away.

Even when a man marries a woman with grown children who are now living on their own, some tensions from steprelationships can still impact the remarriage. For example, the adult children may treat the stepfather as a rival for the estate they expected to inherit. The stepfather may treat the stepchildren's accustomed drop-in visits with their mother as an intrusion in the privacy of his new marriage. In cases where children are younger, a stepfather can still encounter problems he did not sign on for. For example, marrying a woman whose ex-husband has custody of her fifteen-year-old, the stepfather expects to have only occasional visitation contact with his stepchild. Then one day, the father calls to say he can no longer cope with his adolescent and wants to send the troubling child to live with the boy's mother and her new husband. Remarriages with stepchildren must deal with much that was not anticipated.

Born of loss from death or divorce; divided by a host of unfamiliar differences; and beset by conflicts over sharing, loyalty, jealousy, and competition; stepfamilies turn out to be much more challenging to live in than most remarriage partners usually anticipate. High hopes and good intentions are not enough to make this reconstituted family work. There is no point underestimating the difficulties that will be encountered. Realistic understanding is what is needed. The figures don't lie.

Although spousal death terminates a lot of marriages, divorce brings an end to most. About one-half of first marriages divorce. The majority of single partners, many now with children, choose to remarry. *The rate of divorce for remarriages without children is higher than for first marriages, whereas the rate of divorce in remarriages with stepchildren is the highest of all (about 75 percent),* a fact that has been partly attributed to the increased conflicts in steprelationships (see Part Nine).

Many stepfamilies can and do work well, but not without a lot of effort, understanding, tolerance, communication, and restraint. Every member has an important part to play, *with stepfathering being the part under discussion here.* Each Key in this book examines one major facet of this complex and demanding role, by explaining problems to beware of and possibilities that might develop. *To know what to do right depends on understanding what can go wrong.*

In Part One, the stepfather's entry into *instant family* is described and strategies are suggested for easing his own and the children's adjustment. Part Two emphasizes the importance of realigning expectations from wishful to realistic thinking. Part Three describes the mix of unfamiliar differences stepfamilies create, and suggests how the stepfather can respond to those differences to begin building a lasting relationship with the children. Part Four suggests a variety of ways the new husband can begin to define the stepfather role. Part Five examines the significant others with whom the stepfather must now find a way to get along. Part Six suggests strategies to help the stepfather successfully communicate what he wants to say to positive effect. Part Seven deals with the difficult issue of establishing parental authority as a stepfather. Part Eight discusses the management of heightened emotional intensity that tends to characterize many steprelationships. Part Nine gives some approaches for constructively managing conflict. And Part Ten focuses on how to maintain the marriage, the reason why stepfather and wife got together in the first place—because of their love for each other and their desire to share a common future.

Success of the remarriage depends to a significant degree on how the man structures and conducts the relationship with his wife's children. Stepfathering is part of the husbanding he agrees to do, because she marries him not just as a partner, but as a parent as well. It is hoped that this book will help the stepfather keep his *choices constructive*, his *expectations realistic*, his *contributions significant*, and his *returns rewarding*. Because the stepfathering role is maximally demanding when stepchildren are full-time residents within the family (and not just present at visitation), unless otherwise noted, *full-time stepfathering* is what this book is about. Finally, throughout this discussion, enormous importance is placed upon communication; the stepfather is encouraged to talk about problems that normally beset stepfamily life. If, however, the stepfather is not talkative by nature, he can still benefit from this book by using it to understand the complexity of steprelationships, at least preparing himself for the common difficulties that he may encounter.

This book is not intended to be exhaustive. Stepfathering is a complex and challenging responsibility. It is hoped that by examining the issues presented in these pages, some of the difficult areas can be moderated. At the end of this book, there is a list of suggested reading that is strongly recommended. If, however, after having tried additional reading, seriously disruptive stepfamily problems persist, it is best to seek outside counseling help. To let a bad situation get worse does nobody in the family any good.

PART ONE

ADJUSTING TO THE STEPFATHER RELATIONSHIP

1

UNDERSTANDING WHY FEELINGS ARE MIXED

THE ORIGIN OF AMBIVALENCE

The first key to stepfathering is for the new husband to understand the attitudes stepchildren may bring to him as a result of marriage to their mother. Although past connection to a previous family that included their biological father has been broken by death or divorce, the memory of that family and that father is usually much alive and often missed.

If their mother is divorced, then visitations may keep the relationship with their father current. Sometimes, this intermittent contact can make the father even more powerful. Now that the children get to see him only occasionally, they do not take his importance for granted. It is special to see their father. They have a lot of fun together, because he has become the "good-time parent" who may give them nonstop entertainment, undivided attention, and a great outpouring of love. If divorce can increase the power of the noncustodial parent in the children's eyes, death can increase the biological father's power even more. When the family is widowed, the children's longing for their father can become more strongly felt as idealization of the lost parent begins to grow: "My dad was the greatest dad there was. Nobody can ever replace him!"

In either case, children usually carry into their mother's remarriage a primary attachment to their father with which the stepfather should usually not try to compete. *Competition only encourages children to compare the stepfather with their father, loyally concluding that their mother's new husband just can't do things as well, can't be as much fun, or can't matter as deeply as their dad.* Stepfathers who choose to enter this competition are bound to lose. Loyalty to the deceased, honored father or to the fun weekend, dad will prevail.

By actively trying to measure up to their father, the stepfather only inhibits the children's capacity to commit to himself. Then competition can become a trap. "But Dad doesn't do it this way," protest the stepchildren, acting like the stepfather should replicate the conduct of their father. Or they may object: "Why should we do it your way when you're not our father?"

This kind of feedback can alert the stepfather that a distinction needs to be made for his sake, for the stepchildren's sake, and for the sake of their family relationship. He can make this distinction by saying something like this: "I am not here to resemble, replace, keep up with, or improve on your father. I am here to be myself. I am here to act in the role of father in this family in a way that fits for me and ideally will work for you. Don't expect me to be just like your dad. But if some of the differences between me and him are hard to get used to, I hope you will tell me and we can talk about them." Should the stepfather fall into the trap where competition with the father creates an expectation of similarity, declaring independence in his role can help to get him out.

If the stepchildren are extremely young and openhearted, or if the father is long out of touch, the stepfather may enter the relationship with these children unobstructed by this primary attachment. Even so, no matter how much they thought they wanted their mother to remarry, or no matter how much they have come to like her new husband, stepchildren are going to have some *ambivalence* toward their stepfather.

They may feel reluctant to give to a new father figure that filial respect and love belonging to the father they have always known. At first they are at a loss: How are they supposed to treat a stepfather? The terms on which they are supposed to accept him have yet to be worked out. To be told to call the stepfather "Dad," or to be told this man is now their "father," often arouses a lot of unnecessary antipathy. To follow such directives can be threatening to children who may feel like they are being told to betray the loyalty to their existing father, or to the memory of their father who has died. In consequence, they may feel confused, conflicted, and guilty. More important, they may *resent* their stepfather for usurping a role that he has not earned, and in which he does not truly belong.

Because *forcing fatherhood usually creates resistance* by insisting on similarity, it generally works better for the stepfather to enter the family picture with a more open agenda. To create this flexibility, he can say something like this: "Marrying your mother means I agree to assume some responsibility for your care, that I am concerned for your well-being, that I want to get to know you, that I want you to get to know me, and that I want to do what I can to help us get along."

The naming of the stepfather should be left up to the children. If they feel comfortable calling him "Dad," that is fine. Sometimes a preschool child will want to call a stepfather "Daddy" to create the opportunity for closeness comparable to what is or was felt for the biological father. Usually an adolescent will prefer to use the first name to distinguish stepfather from father in order to create an important distinction and a comfortable separation. Operating on a first-name basis with the stepfather is *not* an act of disrespect; it is an effort to acknowledge social familiarity while maintaining adequate emotional distance.

There are other sources of ambivalence as well. Having lived for some period of time just with a single parent, the stepchildren's sharing of their mother with a stepfather can feel like losing primary access to her. In addition, the stepfather also takes up space and makes demands, creating a new presence in the family that at times can feel intrusive. Even though he can be nice and fun to have around, sometimes stepchildren may just wish he would go away.

Ambivalence, however, is not only on the children's side. Like them as he does, there are still moments when the stepfather wishes he could have married his wife free from the encumbrance of her children. This is one reason why the children's visitation with their father is so important. It allows the stepfather and his wife time to be alone. Even the mother is not immune to ambivalence, finding herself at times longing for a simpler existence, where she did not have to juggle the competing demands and conflicting wants of her children and a new husband.

Ambivalence is not a problem in stepfamilies, it is an ongoing reality. It becomes a problem only when the stepfather, stepchildren, or mother refuse to accept the authentic mixture of their feelings toward each other that fatigue or hard times can arouse. *There are simply going to be occasions when the steprelationship is going to feel ambivalent, and that's okay.*

For the stepfather, management of these ambivalent feelings requires taking some affirmative actions so the negative side of his relationship with the stepchildren does not come to dominate his perception of them, driving him into negative behavior in response.

- He needs to accept his negative feelings as natural, although recognizing that they are only part of the total emotional picture. It helps to remember that he has positive feelings for them as well.

- He needs to be able to say to his wife something like this: "At times I find it hard tolerating difficulties with your children, and I need to take a break." She needs to understand that this is his request for a *time-out* (for some space and freedom from responsibility for the children), and not a rejection of stepfatherhood. He just wants some separation to recover perspective. It naturally feels harder to live around and to be involved with children who are not your own.
- When he is ready, he needs to reengage with them in a situation or around an activity where he can get back in touch with the positive side of their relationship, enjoying and appreciating how they are.

If the stepfather can do what he can to keep exposure to the stepchildren within his tolerance for the negative and to create contacts where he can appreciate the positive, then the natural ambivalence he will sometimes feel for them, and they for him, may be more manageable for them all.

2

APPRECIATING THE STEPCHILDREN'S ADJUSTMENT

FROM PARENTAL DIVORCE TO MATERNAL REMARRIAGE

When a man marries a women with chidren, he doubles up on his adjustment. Simultaneously, he must learn to accept the roles of husband and of stepfather. To become a husband was primarily why he wanted to get married: to partner through life the woman whom he loves. Becoming a full-time stepfather was part of the bargain that he willingly accepted (if her child was a resident at the outset), or that he may have reluctantly agreed to (if a custodial father, as often happens, sends a troublesome adolescent back to live with his or her mother). In either case, when the stepfather encounters stepchildren in various stages of *resistance* to accepting him, it can make keeping his part of the bargain more difficult than he anticipated. If he is trying, why can't they?

They are. *Resistance is part of the children's early effort to adjust to their mother's remarriage.* Before they can accept a stepfather's role in their mother's life, they have to let go of how it was with her as a single parent, when they were the primary focus of her concern. A stepfather represents a change in the lives of stepchildren, and it takes time for them to make this transition. *Resistance is how they slow down the rate of their adjustment by keeping the demands for change within tolerable limits.*

Resistance to a new stepfather can take many forms. Stepchildren can act as if he is not there, does not count, or does not belong. They can refuse to make room for his presence, respect his possessions, or accommodate his needs. They can complain to their mother about how much better family life used to be *before* "everything changed," by which they mean adding a stepfather to their number. Hard times now may be deliberately contrasted with good times back then. What's going on?

The mother's new husband and her children used to get on so well before they married and before they all moved in together. And now, when he and their mother are ready to grow happily forward with their new marriage, it feels like the stepchildren are holding them back and dragging them down. Their resistance requires understanding.

Making the Adjustment from Parental Divorce to Maternal Remarriage

Through resisting family change initiated by their parents, not only do children slow down the process of transition, they try to influence some of the outcome to suit their needs. Both goals are important, because going through parental divorce, followed by a period of single-parent family living, and then parental remarriage, all place enormous adjustment demands on children. If the stepfather can be mindful of the following six common adjustments, this understanding can give him perspective on, and patience with, the process of transition through which his stepchildren are moving:

1. Intimacy with a stranger
2. Conditional caring
3. Less attention to go around

4. Additional loss
5. The end of reunion fantasies
6. Seeing parents change

When their biological parents were married, children experienced intimacy among family members. Divorce created distance between their parents and a reduction of intimacy. Depending on a single parent increased intimacy with their mother, but now that she is remarried, living with their stepfather may feel like being thrust into family *intimacy with a stranger.* "It's like living with a man I don't even know," as one self-conscious adolescent described it. "Now I have to watch how I dress and undress in my own home!"

In the children's original family, caring among everyone felt unconditional. Divorce, however, called into question the nature of that caring, at least between their parents, and perhaps of their parents for them. "If Mom and Dad can stop loving each other, can they also stop loving us?" In the family created by their mother's remarriage, *caring for and from their stepfather may feel extremely conditional* because there is no history of love bonding them from birth. "When my stepfather doesn't like how I act, he has no love for me to fall back on." "If I do love him, how do I know he won't go away like my father?" "If he's only temporary, why risk loving him and getting hurt again?" "Maybe the best way to test if he's here to stay is to see if I can make him go away."

In the children's family of origin, it felt like there was enough caring to go around. Divorce, however, showed the loss of caring between their parents, and created a lessening of attention from each parent. Their mother, the custodial parent, had to assume more responsibilities for running the family by herself and so became busier and less accessible. Their father, the non-custodial parent, now saw them only on visitations, and so they had less regular contact with him. Now, with their mother remarried, it feels like there is *more competition for less attention to go around.* "We have to wait for our stepfather to be away if we want time alone with our mother!"

In the children's original family, both of their parents were fully present. With divorce, only one resident parent is left at home, and the children have occasional contact with the one who has moved out. Then, when their mother remarries, it feels as if they have *lost part of the remaining parent* to the time she wants to spend with her new husband alone. "Losing my dad was hard enough, but now it feels like I'm losing my mom, too."

In the original family, children assumed their parents would remain wed forever. This assumption gave a measure of security to the children's sense of future. Divorce decreed that the marriage was dissolved, but the children may still dream that their parents will somehow get reunited. Now, with remarriage, their mother is committing to this new husband, thereby *putting an end to the children's reunion fantasies.* Mom and Dad are definitely not going to get back together. The familiar past is missed, the present becomes confusing, and the unfamiliar future is difficult to accept. "It's hard seeing your parents break up the old family, but it's even harder seeing them start a new family with someone else."

In the original family, the parents seemed to stay the same way the children had always known them. Then with divorce, both parents began making some personal changes in response to the freedom from each other that they had gained. These *changes in parental values, interests, and outside involvements* take some getting used to for the children. Remarriage changes parents even more. Their mother alters herself further in response to how her new husband is, what he likes, and what he believes (just as he changes in response to her). But children only see the alteration in their parent. "He's changed what my mom likes to do and how she parents."

These are only some of the changes through which children struggle as their mother journeys from divorce into remarriage. By becoming sensitive to these adjustments, however, the stepfather can be more understanding of his stepchildren when they become resistant to the new family situation. If he can hold firm and be patient, insisting on his rightful presence but not hardening their resistance by trying to defeat it, he can give the stepchildren some time to adjust. They need this time to work toward an acceptance of his place in their new family life.

If the mother and the stepfather are so inclined, all of the six adjustment difficulties listed above can be discussed openly with stepchildren to achieve a number of beneficial effects.

- Children get to see that the complexity of their adjustment is understood and appreciated.
- Children themselves come to understand that many of the adjustments they face are *not* because something is personally wrong or deficient in them, but because of the nature of the particular transition through which they are passing.
- Children get a chance to discuss additional adjustments that they find challenging. It becomes permissible to experience problems and helpful to talk about them.
- Children, mother, and stepfather can formulate measures that can ease some of these adjustments (i.e., ensuring sufficient privacy for adolescent comfort; creating some time for the children and the mother alone), thereby demonstrating that together they have the power to work out problems.

3
PHASING IN

GOING SLOW AT THE BEGINNING

Coping with change, whether unexpected, chosen, or inevitable, is an ongoing challenge in life. A revolutionary process, change upsets and resets the terms on which people live, taking them out of an *old* reality and placing them into a *new* one.

The adjustments required by major life change can be extremely taxing. First, people struggle to *let go* of an old way of life that is valued and missed, seeing how much can be salvaged and carried forward. Second, they *grope through* a period of uncertainty, at times feeling lost in the transition, unsure of what to do and of what shall happen next. Third, they try to *learn* how to cope with unfamiliar demands created by the different situation they have entered, testing limits to determine their new boundaries. Coping with loss, tolerating confusion, and mastering new skills and understandings are the capacities usually required to cope with major change.

By refusing to let go of the former way of life, people are at risk of forcing on new situations old definitions that simply do not fit. By refusing to accept the new reality, people tend to experience ongoing conflict with their altered circumstance and the people in it. Remarriage with children is a challenging change for every member of the stepfamily, with each one struggling with both kinds of refusal. For everyone, there is a former way of life to leave behind. There is awkwardness from unfamiliarity with new family members. There is an enormous amount to figure out about each other so everyone can get along as the new family takes form and begins to function.

What will stepfamily life be like? This is the question that is on everyone's mind. How will life be the same and how will it be different from what they have known before? It can be helpful for everyone to discuss this question, *identifying positive similarities* that will carry on to create security from continuity, like children remaining in the same school, and *dispelling imaginary differences*, negative in nature, that will not occur, like children losing contact with their father.

Remarriage with children, like many changes in life, is usually a broken promise. For the mother and the stepfather, remarried family life shall not be as idyllic as they may have hoped. For the older stepchildren, it shall not prove as awful as they may have feared.

For the stepfather, the watchword for entering remarriage is: "Go slow, and be careful of the changes that you make." There are three early pitfalls for him to beware, each one resulting in the well-intentioned stepfather appearing to his stepchildren in the stereotyped role of "the evil stepparent." Cinderella's stepmother and David Copperfield's stepfather both convey the mean-spirited, jealous, and tyrannical terms in which this family addition has long been portrayed. These pitfalls are as follows:

1. Demanding too much change of his stepchildren at first and appearing tyrannical.
2. Supporting his wife's mothering at the expense of their marriage at first, and then *becoming possessive* of her in response.
3. Overgiving to his stepchildren at first to make those relationships work and *ending up resentful.*

The Evil Stepfather as "Tyrannical"

When an entering stepfather immediately insists on instituting new, improved parenting routines that must be followed and rules that must be obeyed, he is in danger of prematurely arousing opposition that may interfere with the stepchildren getting to know and accept him. It is better to go with the flow of family functioning for a while, letting family members grow accustomed to his character and habits before beginning to assert his wants for family change. By forcing more influence than the relationship yet has trust or comfort to bear, his will shall be resisted. When conflict results, he appears to his stepchildren as a man who cares more about having his way than caring to know them. *Better for him to fit in and become familiar first, and then gradually make changes later.*

The Evil Stepfather as "Possessive"

Loving his wife and wanting to support her relationship with the children during this period of transition, the stepfather may offer to set his own needs and those of the marriage aside for the sake of family. Taking him at his word, his wife devotes herself to the children's adjustment needs, until it suddenly seems to the stepfather that she has little time and concern left for him. Feeling lonely and disconnected in his new marriage, he becomes jealous of his wife's primary attention to the children that he encouraged. He feels threatened by their competition. Wanting more of his wife's time to get their marriage back, he begins to act possessive of her, treating the stepchildren as enemy to that interest. *He would have been better served by keeping the marriage solidified from the outset, rather than self-sacrificing and later feeling insecure.*

The Evil Stepfather as "Resentful"

Wanting to get along with his stepchildren, the stepfather may try too hard by courting their approval, by being amenable to their every request, and by pleasing and being generous to a fault. Because he is the only stepfather they have known, the stepchildren accept all they are given without restraint, taking it for granted, and taking without giving back, because he is careful to make no demands for a return from them. Soon he gives beyond what he can emotionally afford. He feels hurt and exploited by the lack of mutuality in the relationship. Feeling taken advantage of, he grows angry, withdraws what he has been giving, and acts resentful. *He would have been better served had he given less and asked for more at the beginning, structuring a relationship with them that was two-sided, not one.*

Where the tyrannical stepfather demands too much from stepchildren at first, the resentful stepfather asks too little. At issue is finding a middle way: giving within reasonable limits and requesting some reciprocity in return. "Go slow at the beginning" means the stepfather should

- first become familiar with the family flow before trying to change it;
- keep the needs of the developing marriage a top priority;
- and not overgive to stepchildren to get along.

4

THE COMPROMISE
THEORY OF
RELATIONSHIP

WHY GETTING ALONG OKAY IS GOOD ENOUGH

All relationships, not only steprelationships, are complicated because of certain built-in tensions that, no matter how well managed, will never go away. By understanding the *mix* of these tensions, a stepfather can keep relationships, both with his wife and with his stepchildren, working as well as possible. In the process, he will come to appreciate why over time no relationship, no matter how beloved, is perfect. Instead, each is constructed from a *mixture* of components that sometimes will compete and conflict. When this clash occurs, a compromise must be struck among these components. This compromise itself is oftentimes the best relationship anyone can get.

What is this mixture of components? There are three— *rewards, responsibilities,* and *risks*—and they all coexist in each stepfamily relationship that remarriage has created. Consider the marriage itself.

Rewards

When the stepfather chose to marry the mother of these children, and she chose to marry him, they wed to gain certain *rewards* from their relationship to sustain their love. These rewards are of two kinds, both *enhancing caring feelings* for each other. First, each wanted to *give* of themselves in ways they valued to the other person—by sharing, by responding, by supporting, by affection, and by play, among others. And second, each wanted to *get* certain rewards in return—listening, confiding, companionship, collaboration, attention, and appreciation, among others.

The rewards of caring are many and varied, with each partner differing in those he or she values most. Of the two kinds, however, those from *giving* are the ones each partner can control. Those from *getting* are up to the other person. Because there is no mind reading, letting the other person know what expressions of caring feel most meaningful to receive is extremely important to communicate. "If you really loved me, you'd know what mattered to me without having to be told" is a romantic fantasy. It is not usually true.

For the stepfather and his new wife, the priority of keeping this exchange of rewards ongoing cannot be overstated. When distraction with jobs, children, and family matters causes the giving and getting of marital rewards to go unattended, then omission will cause the relationship to suffer from neglect.

Although love may be unconditional, feelings of caring and being cared for are not. They depend on this continual exchange of rewards for demonstration and affirmation. To maintain the quality of married life, the stepfather needs to do what he can to keep the exchange of rewards as high as he can.

Responsibilities

In a committed, caring relationship like marriage, there is no free love. Neither partner can reap only rewards. Each must incur a *cost,* and neither welcomes the expense. To get valued rewards, some *personal freedom* is relinquished. Thus, the compromise begins. This cost is unavoidable because part of their commitment is *responsibility* for the well-being of the partner and their relationship. These responsibilities are of two kinds. First there are *obligations*—efforts both partners must make for the sake of the relationship like keeping each other adequately informed, sharing significant decisions that affect them both, performing household chores, and contributing income, among others. Second, there are *prohibitions*—restraints that both partners must abide for the sake of the relationship, like not breaking confidences, not having outside affairs, and not indebting the other without first gaining agreement, among others.

For the stepfather, the most apparent and burdensome responsibility is usually simply living with the daily reality of his wife's children. If he has led a bachelor existence up to now, marriage entails a loss of personal freedom to his wife *and* to her children. When this extreme adjustment is the case, the stepfather needs an adequate flow of rewards in the marriage to outweigh the cost of responsibility that comes with this family change. At the same time, he needs to moderate the amount of freedom he gives up, by limiting the responsibility he will take for her children, keeping it within a tolerable range.

Whereas loss of rewards can tend to reduce feelings of caring, unrecompensed loss of personal freedom can arouse feelings of anger. The stepfather may sometimes feel: "It's not right, it's not fair that her children take so much of our money, demand so much of our time, and interfere so much in our marriage." Now the compromise is truly felt. And when it is, the couple needs to honestly assess and reallocate the costs of responsibility, as well as taking time together to reaffirm the rewards of their marriage.

How do the stepfather and his wife balance rewards with responsibilities in their marriage? By agreeing to keep adjusting their relationship as personal and circumstantial change continually alters the mix of these two components, each partner is committed to coming up with new compromises both can support.

Risks

The compromise of relationship, however, goes beyond attaching responsibilities to rewards because there are also *risks* each partner takes. As a function of their love, each becomes sensitive, open, and vulnerable to the other. Those we love the most can hurt us the worst. So if the compromise dictates that rewards yield personal satisfaction, and responsibilities limit personal freedom, then risks raise the possibility of personal harm, of *getting hurt.*

There are possible hurts from treatments of two kinds. Acts of *commission* and acts of *omission* can both cause pain. What the other person *does do* can inflict injury. For example, aroused by conflict, the husband or the wife may cruelly attack with cutting words or sullenly withdraw beyond the reach of communication. What the other person *does not do* can create suffering. Preoccupied with work or under stress, the husband or the wife may not listen, forget a promise, or overlook an anniversary.

In stepfamilies, particularly those just getting started, it is important for the stepfather to understand how most offenses that are given are unintentional, the natural outcome of being ignorant of one another. Getting to know each other has a lot to do with getting to learn how each other can be hurt. Getting along with each other has a lot to do with *consideration*—not repeating certain acts of commission or omission after being told they are a cause for pain.

How Stepchildren Affect the Compromise in Marriage

The stepfather needs to be particularly realistic about his relationship to his stepchildren, which can often feel extremely mixed. As long as the rewards of caring remain high with his stepchildren, the stepfather willingly sacrifices personal freedom for their sake, assuming parental responsibility and being forgiving when inevitable hurts occur. As his rewards diminish, however, as they often do when stepchildren enter adolescence and become more self-centered and less considerate, his caring for them can become eroded, his tolerance for parental responsibility can go down, and his sensitivity to little injuries from what they do and do not do can go up.

As this mix with his stepchildren worsens, his relationship with his wife can be affected. Rather than blame her for how the children are behaving, however, this is a time for him to talk with her about the unsatisfactory mix of rewards, responsibilities, and risks he is feeling in his relationship with them. This is a time for the husband and the wife to discuss changes that might be made by each of them and by the children that could bring that relationship back into his tolerable range.

Then, there will be crises with her children that cause the mother to commit to parenting at the expense of the marriage, with the stepfather losing some rewards of her companionship for a period of time. In consequence, his motivation to gladly assume his share of responsibilities for the stepchildren (who now appear as enemies to his marriage) may diminish, whereas his irritability with their normal habits may be raised. The less rewarding the marriage feels, the less give he may have for the stepchildren. This is why in a remarriage with children, the mother and the stepfather are well advised to keep maintenance of their marriage a top priority. *A strong remarriage can tolerate a lot of difficulty with stepchildren. A weak remarriage cannot.*

The stepfather's goal with his wife, and particularly with his stepchildren, needs to be *to maximize the rewards, to moderate the responsibilities,* and *to minimize the risks.* Anytime the compromise begins to feel like a "bad bargain"—the responsibilities and risks outweighing the rewards—he and his wife need to communicate how this feels, and decide what they can do to restructure the mix of components in their relationship in order to restore the well-being of both partners.

How Authority Worsens the Compromise

Early in remarriage, it is extremely important for the stepfather to let his wife take lead authority with the stepchildren when correction is required. By doing otherwise, he can negatively set the mix of his relationship with them before a positive base of familiarity has been adequately established. Parental discipline typically takes three forms:

1. *Rewards* like privileges may be withdrawn.
2. *Responsibilities*, like limitations on freedom, may be imposed.
3. Sometimes, even *risks* from verbal or physical punishment may be endured.

In any of these cases, the errant child or adolescent is not happy with the adult discharging that authority.

Because the mother has a long and positive history with the children, it is better for her to initially assume this thankless role. The children accept the negative from her because they know it is founded on a positive base of love. The stepfather, however, shall need time to build a foundation of acceptance with his stepchildren. Only then can he begin to exercise corrective authority without risking injury to their relationship. (For a more extensive discussion of establishing stepfather authority, see Keys 26–28.)

PART TWO

CLARIFYING EXPECTATIONS ABOUT STEPFATHERING

5

ROMANTIC IS NOT REALISTIC

ADJUSTING EXPECTATIONS TO FIT THE WAY THINGS ARE

Emphasizing the positives, falling in love encourages *romantic thinking* that often subscribes to certain articles of faith. There is a sense of *destiny*: "Our relationship was meant to be." There is a sense of *empowerment*: "Our love shall conquer all." There is a sense of *optimism*: "We shall live happily ever after." This affirmative outlook is usually part of what persuades people into marriage and, even should it fail to last, does not discourage more romantic thinking when remarriage occurs, as it often does after widowhood or divorce. Love is usually blind to some degree, delighting in the pleasures of romance and denying the potential problems of reality.

Although romantic thoughts, feelings, and gestures are still needed to nourish the relationship after marriage, there must be an operational shift in thinking if the couple is to move from falling in love at the outset to growing in love over time. For their union to last, *realistic thinking* must take hold as they engage with the day-to-day challenges of what is required for two people to share a life together.

Consider some mathematics in marriage relationships. In a two-person union, the simplest relationship, only two lines of interaction must be managed—the husband initiating an exchange with his wife and her responding, and the wife initiating an exchange with her husband and him responding. Add a child, and the number of possible exchanges increases to six (each partner with the other = two, each partner with the child = two, the child with each parent = two), whereas adult roles expand from simply being marriage partners to now becoming mother and father. Add two children, and the number of lines of possible family exchanges to be managed rises to twelve, with the system becoming more arithmetically complex with the addition of each family member. Why consider such numbers?

Because, remarrying with a child or children is *not* a simple marriage. The sheer number of possible interactions increases family complexity not only mathematically, but *psychologically* and *behaviorally* as well. There is the additional challenge of reconciling and integrating historical, affectional, and social differences in the stepfamily, and the presence and influence of ex-spouses and ex-in-laws to be taken into account. In the face of all this perplexity, the *wishful thinking* of romance needs to give way to the *practical thinking* of how to make the stepfamily reality work.

The first step in realistic thinking is to clarify some *expectations* that fit the dynamics of remarriage with stepchildren so the couple can effectively cope with the complexity they have created. Expectations are simply mental sets people construct in the present to help anticipate the future and prepare for what comes next. As long as the reality people expect is roughly equivalent to the reality they encounter, the transition into a new and different situation feels okay. Armed with this realistic preparation, a stepfather can honestly say: "I never thought marrying a woman with children would be simple or easy, so I was ready for some family problems to occur."

The drawback of romantic thinking is that it creates unrealistic expectations about stepfamily life that are usually violated to everyone's cost. For example, suppose the children expect that the new family *will* be run exactly along the same lines as the old single-parent family. Suppose the mother *wants* the stepfather and the children to immediately bond and love each other. Suppose the stepfather expects that the children *should* be willing to accept his authority without question or complaint.

The initial experience with stepfamily life usually violates these expectations. When the children's *prediction* that the new family will be run just like the old is not met, they may experience *surprise and anxiety.* Their stepfather has different beliefs about a family than their father does, and a different operating style as a parent. When the mother's *ambition* that the stepfather and the children immediately come to love each other as she loves them all is not met, she may experience *disappointment and grief.* Sometimes her new husband and her own children don't get on, occasionally acting like they don't even like each other. When the stepfather's *condition* that the children should obey his limits and demands is not met, he may experience a sense of *betrayal and anger.* Quite reasonably, the children act like he is some outsider coming into their lives to exercise parental authority to which he is not historically entitled. *Unrealistic expectations slow down the process of adjustment.*

Like other major life transitions, getting a new stepfamily defined and running takes about two years. A lot of trial-and-error learning on everyone's part is required before they all become adjusted. The new family will not operate exactly as the old. Stepfather and stepchildren will not necessarily immediately bond in love. The stepfather's authority is usually not immediately accepted at the outset.

These are just a few of the realities that can be anticipated in the early development of stepfamily life. None of these early expectations, however, mean that *in time* the new family cannot come to function well, that *in time* stepfather and stepchildren cannot come to care about and love one another, and that *in time* the stepfather's authority cannot become established and respected. The key expectation here is this: *Adjustment takes time.*

To help this adjustment along, the stepfather and the new wife need to first clarify with each other and then with the children a set of realistic expectations to get them started. They can do this by discussing and defining three kinds of expectations with the children.

1. "What do we think stepfamily life will be like?" (What are our *predictions?*)
2. "What do we want stepfamily life to be like?" (What are our *ambitions?*)
3. "What do we believe stepfamily life should be like?" (What are our *conditions?*)

By each member of the family getting these expectations out in the open, unrealistic expectations can be exposed and dispelled, thereby reducing some likelihood of violation and emotional distress.

Then the stepfather can elicit expectations about his role held by other members of the family, using these data to create an entry definition that fits the reality of his own and other people's needs. A possible statement of that definition could sound like this: "Your mother will be the parent to usually go to when you have questions about rules or need permission. She will also be the parent to give any correction. At the beginning, I want to follow her lead and take time so you and I can come to know each other better. Please treat me not as someone who is here to replace your actual father, but as someone who wants to gradually learn how to act in the role of father in this family."

Not all expectations can be clarified through discussion. There will still be some violated expectations for everyone when the stepfamily is first created. Feelings of frustration and anger will be expressed as emotional *protest* ("This isn't right, this shouldn't be, this isn't fair!") and as *resistance* ("I won't go along, I refuse to give in, why should I?"). People don't adjust to major life change with the flick of a psychological switch. Adjustment is an emotional struggle. Clarifying realistic expectations helps, but so does being tolerant as each stepfamily member works through his or her own particular set of violations that make this new reality difficult for them to accept. Therefore, it helps if the stepfather can keep these points in mind:

- *Protest* helps release pain associated with giving up an old way of living;
- *resistance* helps slow down and perhaps modify the demands of the new way of living;
- and *clarification* helps family members begin to develop a frame of reference that fits the reality of stepfamily life.

Better not to shut protest up, but to listen to it. Better not to punish resistance, but to be firm and patient in response. And better not to ignore expectations, but to elicit them and dispel those that are unrealistic.

6

BREAKING IN

WHEN THE SINGLE-PARENT FAMILY
IS LONG ESTABLISHED

How long the mother has lived as a single parent, after divorce, widowhood, or abandonment, can have a powerful bearing on how receptive children are to a stepfather's entry into their lives. In general, the more years the mother and the children have been living as a single-parent family unit:

- the more *habituated* children become to their roles, rules, and routines;
- the more *reliant* they become on unobstructed access to their mother;
- and the more *proprietary* they become in their relationship to her.

As they defend what they are used to, as they insist on the old availability of their mother, and as they protect the special relationships they have developed with her, an entering stepfather may encounter resistance from his stepchildren on all three fronts.

In the wake of losing their father as a daily member in their immediate family, a rebonding of children to the last remaining parent—their mother—usually occurs. In service of security, support, and survival, interdependence draws the mother and her children closer than they were before. They come to depend on her to provide some of that nurturance and to fulfill some of those functions that were part of their father's contribution when he was present. On her side, the mother comes to depend on them to undertake increased responsibility for themselves and to do more upkeep of the household.

This new interdependence can also create a quality of adult-like closeness between the mother and the children when she sometimes relies on them for social companionship and they learn to act older in response, often feeling good about this precocity. The more "adult" children come to feel in relationship to their mother—the son perhaps feeling like he has become "the man of the house," the daughter perhaps feeling she has become her "mother's best friend"—the less need either child sees for the addition of another adult, a stepfather, to their family. Reluctant to let go of the special roles they have assumed, the stepchildren may blame the stepfather for their loss.

Children who grow to take adult possession of their mother may resist letting that possession go. Their mother can also experience considerable conflict. She wants to honor the relationship with the man she is marrying, but feels guilty pushing the children away to make the necessary room. The stepfather can help his wife with this emotionally complex transition by giving assurance that by loving him she is not required to abandon care for them, and that he values her for the parental love she gives. He may also explain that their remarriage can be in the long-term interest of the children's growth: In consequence of her attachment to him, they shall feel more free to separate from her and develop primary relationships of their own. Now her son does not have to be the man of the house. Now the daughter does not have to be her mother's best friend. Their mother's remarriage releases them to seek significant friendships and establish social independence without being held back by burdensome "adult" responsibility for her.

Because the degree of rebonding between mother and children tends to be proportional to how many years they have functioned alone, the stepfather needs to anticipate some resistance when he breaks into a long-standing single-parent family unit. To moderate this resistance, there are some actions he can take to ease his acceptance into the family.

Ways to Reduce Resistance

- In response to the children's *habituation* to the old way of running the family, his entry is best served by fitting into existing family functioning, first; building a relationship with the children, second; talking with his wife about any changes he would like to make, third; and (with her support) gradually introducing those changes, fourth. The stepfather needs to build a foundation of acceptance with the children before beginning to initiate a lot of modifications.

- In response to their sole *reliance* on their mother, the stepfather can make himself available so the stepchildren can also come to rely on him for some of what they want. Now there is more family support when they have need. When their mother is unavailable, they can call on him.

- In response to the children feeling *proprietary* of their mother, the stepfather can help them learn to share her attention by assuring them that her love for him in no way diminishes her love for them. She is still steadfastly there when they have need. *There is still enough love to go around. Less time with her does not mean less love from her.*

- In joint consultation, mother and stepfather can introduce enjoyable activities and begin new family traditions that were not available to the children in the single-parent family. After all, change not only creates loss and demands adjustments, but creates new opportunities as well.

- The mother and the stepfather can set aside special times when the children can still be alone with her without him. Remarriage doesn't mean children have to give up all exclusive contact with their mother.

- Most powerfully, the mother and the stepfather can create times when she is absent from the family, leaving him and the children to develop their new relationship alone. This is time to get to know each other, to recreate and work together without her presence to distract them from each other. This early exposure shows them what it's like when he's in charge, allowing the children to become more familiar with him as a parent, as they look to him for structure and guidance, and come to him when needs and wants arise.

7

BONDING OR BINDING

AGES OF THE STEPCHILDREN
CAN MAKE A DIFFERENCE

Certain variables tend to affect how quickly and how closely stepchildren bond with their stepfather: the degree to which the biological father is actively present in the children's life is one; the age of the children at the time of maternal remarriage is another.

In general, if the biological father is absent without contact, then the stepfather may come to occupy a vacant role in the family that younger stepchildren want filled. A very active biological father, however, creates a presence that requires the stepfather to make a clear distinction. To the stepchildren, he can declare something like this: "Even though I am married to your mother and will help with the parenting in the *home,* I am not here to replace your father in your *heart."* Unless this separation is clearly stated, children of any age may feel obliged to withhold acceptance from the stepfather out of loyalty to their father.

Their age also can make a difference in the degree of acceptance and affection the stepchildren feel free to give their stepfather. If they are still in childhood (younger than nine or ten years old), family remains the center of their social world, and doing something with a parent is often chosen over doing something with a friend. At this early age, children can be very receptive to a stepfather who is one more caring adult with whom they can enjoy a relationship and the family. "Mom likes being with him, and so do I."

As a sign of their desire to bring the stepfather into a role of familiarity with them, little children may call him "Dad" or "Daddy," a form of address that often angers older adolescent siblings who may consider this a clear betrayal: "Don't call him 'Dad' when he's not your father!" Adolescent children (over age nine or ten) are less likely to bond with the stepfather, who needs to be very clear why this is so, and not take personally what is usually developmentally ordained.

Divorce Tends to Intensify Adolescence

Frequently perceived by adolescents as a selfish decision made by parents for their own happiness at the expense of what children want, divorce often causes teenagers to become more self-centered in return: "If they don't care about my feelings, then why should I care about theirs?" Adding this "wrong" to their store of existing adolescent grievances against adult authority, in opposition to which some rebellion has probably begun, they may become increasingly resentful. They may exploit this perceived unfairness to justify becoming more ruthless and manipulative on their own behalf. Already in a state of some resentment and resistance with their mother, they are less disposed than younger siblings to welcome the daily presence of a stepfather into their lives, sometimes transferring sullen negativity to him. Because the stepfather did not do anything to earn this cold reception, he need not take it as a personal offense, but give the adolescent a chance to warm up to their relationship, a change that may or may not occur.

Remarriage Accelerates the Adolescent Push for Independence

Even though adolescents may like their stepfather and even though they may want their mother to remarry and be happy, by having her commit to a competing love relationship, they lose some primary attachment to her. In response, teenagers may decide to do what they feel their mother did to them, and place more importance on outside relationships. They may increase their separation from the family in search of more significant relationships with peers, doing this sooner and more intensely than they otherwise might in consequence of the remarriage. "If he's more important to her than us, then my friends are more important to me than my family!"

Socially dependent on their friends and distant at home, these adolescents also become more frustrated when parental rules constrain their freedom to build a social world apart from the family. In addition, seeing their mother affectionately connected and sexually alive with a man who is not their father can feel awkward, and even seem wrong. "I know they're married, but even so, I don't like it when they hug. Everything's changed. Home doesn't feel like home anymore. When I can't get away, I'm more comfortable staying in my room than coming out and pretending to be a family."

Although very young children may be prepared to bond with the stepfather, adolescents are more likely to balk if pushed by their mother or stepfather to establish comparable closeness. Therefore, with teenage stepchildren, the stepfather should respect their need for distance while insisting they respect his right to be in the family as a function of remarriage to their mother. The stepfather should resolve to treat them in a courteous and friendly manner and enjoy them when he can, making several points extremely clear:

- He is committed to their mother and she to him.
- He is not going away.
- He cares about what happens to them.
- He will contribute to their care both as a parent and provider.
- He understands that because they are older, adolescent stepchildren may find it more difficult to gladly accept his addition to the family.

8

BEING A STEPFATHER TO COUNT ON

CREATING A RELIABLE PRESENCE IN FAMILY LIFE

While the stepfather is setting realistic expectations about his entry into stepfamily life, he also needs to consider how to help his wife's children set realistic expectations about him. He can influence those expectations based on the early conduct he presents.

For stepchildren to accept, respect, care for, and perhaps come to love their stepfather, *trust* of him must be established first. *Is he going to be a family member on whom they can count?* If so, they can begin to openly communicate and start attaching to him. Trust derives from their judgment of his *reliability* based on certain categories of his behavior they commonly evaluate.

Comfort

Most fundamental of all is that the stepfather must act in ways that pose no danger to his stepchildren. *They need to feel safe in his presence.* This means he must set limits on how he acts in two dimensions of their relationship: In *conflict* and in *intimacy* with them, he must be careful to inspire no feelings of threat.

No matter how irritating he sometimes finds their company, and no matter how strongly he disapproves of their actions, when inevitable mistakes and misdeeds occur, he will not verbally attack or physically injure them in response. No matter how much he likes them, and no matter how close he wants to get to them, they need have no fear of inappropriate expressions of sexual interest or physical touch by him. *To be comfortable with their new stepfather, the stepchildren need to feel assured that there is no danger, through the expression of misguided anger or affection, of him doing them harm.*

Clarity

Because so much about who and how he is feels unfamiliar to the stepchildren now that they are all living together, daily exposure to him takes some getting used to. In the normal ups and downs of life, it is easy for them to misread his state of mind when they are feeling insecure or he is looking unhappy. It is easy for them to misunderstand his moods when he is feeling stressed and acting noncommunicative, and to misappropriate responsibility for his feelings. It is easy for them to jump to false conclusions and suppose what is not so. "Since he didn't say hello when I got home, he must be angry at something I did. Or maybe he's disappointed because I didn't act the way he wanted." (When in fact, he has just had a difficult day at work and only wants a little time alone to recover.)

Mind reading usually distorts the truth, because people use their own imaginings to explain what they do not know about each other's mental or emotional state. It is better to check their stepfather out when they are in doubt by asking him how he feels or what he is thinking.

Because the relationship is new, however, the stepchildren may not feel confident enough to take this initiative. *Therefore, the stepfather can helpfully keep them informed about the state of his experience.* Coming home from the job an hour late and exhausted, he declares: "I've had a really rough day and need a little time alone to unwind before we get together." Adequate communication counts for a lot.

Consistency

It makes a difference to stepchildren whether their stepfather establishes a predictable pattern of behavior when he joins the family or whether his conduct is unpredictable from one day to the next. In the first case, they can begin to relax around him, being able to anticipate how he is going to act and react. In the second, they are kept off balance, feeling anxious around him much of the time.

His power of consistency contributes to family stability in a variety of important ways. By providing additional parenting support for them, marital support for their mother, and financial support for the family, and by keeping up these efforts over time, he strengthens the adult base of family functioning upon which the well-being of the stepchildren depends.

The frequency of crises that used to occur when single-parent family demands stretched their mother beyond her limits is now reduced because another resident adult is ready and willing to pick up a share of the load. Emergencies, when they do occur, are often less disruptive. "Things have evened out a lot since Mom remarried. Even though home is different, it feels more settled down."

Commitment

One watchword for the stepfather is to be cautious about making commitments to stepchildren that he cannot realistically keep. It can be tempting to prematurely agree to their request for something they want done tomorrow or later in the week, because by pleasing them, they will be pleased with him. However, when unforeseen complications make it necessary for him to break his promise, not only does he disappoint their expectation, but he creates the impression that he does not mean what he says.

When in doubt about his capacity to deliver on what they want him to do, he is better served not by an automatic "Yes," but by a cautious "Maybe; I'll have to wait until then and see."

With children in general, and with stepchildren in particular, it is easier to correct a "no" at the time with a "yes" later on, than to retract a "yes" at the time for a "no" later. In the first case, the correction is seen as a happy surprise, in the second as an unfair betrayal. *By keeping his commitments to them, he becomes a man of his word who means what he says and will not let them down.*

Completion

Whereas commitment promises, "I will do for you what I said," completion declares, "I will finish with you what I start." The power of completion is that it bears directly on the stepfather's *involvement* with his stepchildren. Suppose they ask for his help on some homework. He begins, gets interrupted by a phone call, and then neglects to get back to work with them again. To start a project with them, of their or his own initiation, and then to pull out partway through, not only lets the stepchildren down, but signifies *disinterest.* Whether in providing assistance or engaging in a discussion, follow-through literally *means a lot*. It shows that the step-father really wants to be involved.

To help set affirmative expectations of his role in the step-children's life, the stepfather can model *reliability* by communicating these points:

- "I will be *safe* to be around."
- "I will keep you *adequately informed* about how I am feeling and why."
- "I will contribute *continuity of effort* to increase support of this family."
- "I will *honor any promises* to you I make."
- "I will *finish with you* whatever we have agreed to start doing together."

PART THREE

BEGINNING TO BUILD
RELATIONSHIPS

9

THINKING ABOUT
DIVERSITY

APPROACHING DIFFERENCES IN STEPRELATIONSHIPS

W hen a man marries a woman with children, he increases the mix of human differences in her family, because he is neither as biologically nor as historically similar to them as they have grown to be with each other. Conversely, the addition of these steprelationships increases diversity in his own life as well.

In human relationships—be they social, organizational, or familial—the management of diversity presents ongoing challenges for all parties involved. Exposure to unfamiliar differences can feel estranging, offending, or even threatening. Social separation or conflict is often the result. Differences in tastes, in patterns of conduct, in perceptions, and in beliefs all demand a lot of adaptation. Efforts to understand the new and different, to adjust to what cannot be changed, and to manage disagreement are constantly required.

These challenges apply to steprelationships as well. Sharing a common biological and social heritage with their mother causes children to be more accepting of differences between themselves and her than of those between themselves and their stepfather. Sharing a committed marital love with his wife causes the stepfather to be more attracted to, and accepting of, differences between himself and her than of those between himself and her children. *In a stepfamily, the hardest area of interpersonal diversity to tolerate and manage is between the stepparent and the stepchildren, because they have neither the advantage of a common family history nor the compatibility of marital love to soften the impact of contrasting traits between them.*

In a family created by remarriage, differences between the stepparent and stepchildren are naturally going to be the most abrasive. Prepared for this reality, the stepfather can set the example and lead the way about how individual differences can helpfully be treated. Before considering what approach he should take, it is useful to identify three approaches the stepfather should studiously *avoid:*

1. *"You are different from me,* but if you become like me we will get along."

   Here he makes his acceptance of them conditional on their becoming similar to him, an offer they interpret as demanding *conformity* or receiving *rejection.*

2. *"I am different from you,* but I will set those differences aside and try to become like you so we will get along."

   Here he offers self-denial and imitation as ways of courting their acceptance, an offer they interpret as *approval seeking* and a *lack of authenticity.*

3. *"There are no significant differences between us,* therefore we will focus only on similarities in order to get along."

   Here he refuses to acknowledge valued differences between himself and them, a difference-blind approach they interpret either as *discounting diversity* they consider important, or *avoiding diversity* because it is potentially divisive.

   The significance of human differences in relationships is that they set people apart as individuals. People want their individuality respected because it is a statement of their uniqueness. The reason "the pillars of the temple stand apart" in healthy relationships is because sufficient separateness is needed to support togetherness. Deny human differences in any of the three preceding ways, and the relationship between all parties becomes inadequately differentiated and oppressive. "We will live on my terms only." "We will live on your terms only." "We will live on terms that disallow any differences between us only." This is why the fourth approach to individual differences is the only functional one for the stepfather to follow:

4. *"We are all different from each other,* and from this diversity we can create a source of richness from which all of us can benefit."

Here the stepfather not only affirms the value of what everyone has to contribute, but places stepfamily diversity in a positive light. *The key to making steprelationships work well is to treat increased family diversity not as a liability, but as an advantage that creates exposures, experiences, and understandings that can enrich the lives of everyone concerned.*

So much for theory. The next Key considers how a stepfamily can put this theory to the test.

10

MOVING IN TOGETHER

GETTING PRACTICAL ABOUT DIVERSITY

Consider what first happens when two separate households are combined into one. Moving in together is an *initiation*. It allows stepfamily members to *specifically* and *symbolically* begin accommodating to new differences by literally and figuratively "making room for each other" in their daily lives.

Almost immediately, unfamiliar and opposing differences become abrasive and collide, particularly if everyone agrees to live in one partner's residence or the other's (although moving into a neutral space is still no sanctuary from this conflict). To be comfortable in new surroundings, the moving-in party (or parties), accompanied by furnishings and other personal belongings, and accustomed to certain household rules, responsibilities, and lifestyle routines, wants to claim some individual space, expects to share common resources, and plans to assert a family presence in order to feel comfortable in the other partner's home.

Suppose the moving-in party is the stepfather. He is coming to live in his wife's apartment or house that before remarriage barely had room for her and the two teenagers who feel like their traditional space is being invaded by an outsider, which in a way it is. How easy for them to feel resentful and protective, and for him to feel apologetic and unwelcome.

As more crowding is created, differences are seen up close. He never knew that adolescents could spend an hour in the bathroom, with a radio blaring through the door, playing raucous music harsh to his ears, while the shower runs on and on. The adolescents never knew their stepfather was into old-fashioned music, had a need for keeping everything picked up, and cared about lowering utility bills by limiting the use of hot water. Their mother did not anticipate that small situations and incidents could loom so irritatingly large, nor that she would be cast in the role of mediator to help work out disagreements and listen to complaints from parties on each side of the steprelationship about each other.

"We are all different from each other" needs to be a watchword, defining entry living arrangements that respect diversity, while working out adjustments, so that everyone can get along. *The first rule in managing diversity is not to criticize or punish differences with which you do not agree.* If the stepfather judges the teenagers' long showers as "wasteful" and labels the children as "irresponsible," that is likely to encourage labeling in return. If not to him directly, they may complain to their mother that he is "uptight" and acting like a "neat freak."

Now the differences between them have become emotionally inflamed by name-calling, with everyone acting like they've been insulted, which they have. *The role of the stepfather in taking the lead and setting the tone for how differences shall be perceived, treated, and resolved is one of the major contributions he can make to stepfamily life.* So when he acts as though differences are normal and are to be respected and expected, are not to be demeaned, and are no one's fault, stepchildren can relax and feel safe joining with him in the ongoing business of working out inevitable disagreements.

To reach accommodation, everyone will need to make some *concessions,* make some *compromises,* and invent some *creative alternatives* that can resolve contrasting views and conflicting needs when they arise.

- Concession requires giving in to some unfamiliar or objectionable differences that people may not like, but are willing to get used to for the sake of harmony in their relationship. So the stepfather gives in to overbearing music that is unmusical to his ears at home, whereas the stepchildren give in to hearing boring music that is unmusical to their ears when riding in his car. Adult and adolescents agree to accept tastes in the other that are not likely to change, to some degree being broadened by what they hear. In most relationships, people learn to work around more differences than they work through, and making concessions is how this is done.

- Compromise means working through a disagreement over a difference to meet the other person halfway, reaching a solution both can support. So the stepchildren agree to cut their showers down to fifteen minutes, which is shorter than the thirty they would like but longer than the five-minute shower the stepfather believes should be sufficient. In one sense, compromise is a losing proposition, with both sides getting less than 100 percent of what each would ideally like. Compromise is a winning proposition, however, in that it shows each party is willing to set aside some self-interest for the good of a relationship that has beneficial value for them both.

- Creative alternatives are those that allow people to invent solutions that often go beyond the bounds of the either/or polarity, beyond simply meeting in the middle between opposing choices. In this case, the wife and mother begins this novel approach to manage the differences between her new husband and her children about the issue of household order. First, she *reframes* the difference: "Neat or messy is not what either of you is really concerned about. What you both want is a degree of order in your surroundings that allows you to feel relaxed." Turning to them:

"Your stepfather needs more order to feel relaxed when he comes home." Turning to him: "Your stepchildren need less order to feel relaxed at home. Neither one of you is right or wrong. We just need to work out a way to live together that can be relaxing for everyone." Following this approach, a proposal then occurs to the stepfather that neither he nor the children had considered. "Why don't we partition our space into always-cleaned-up areas like the living room and kitchen, and sometimes-cleaned-up areas like the children's bedrooms. At least, let's give this kind of system a try." And then they all join in to discuss how such an arrangement might actually be designed.

Diversity becomes a source of richness and cohesiveness when people work around, through, and outside their differences to construct agreements that allow them to live harmoniously together. The stepfather can take the lead in this unifying process by making clear:

- He will not shy away from differences (they are nothing to be afraid of).
- He will not demean differences (they are not to be criticized).
- He will not deny differences (they are to be acknowledged).
- He will work with whatever differences exist or arise in the family (they can be resolved in a satisfactory manner for all concerned).

11

NO-FAULT COLLISIONS

**RESOLVING INCOMPATIBILITIES
WITHIN THE MARRIAGE**

To keep parental reactions to children from spreading divisiveness into the marriage, the stepfather and the mother need to understand how they can evaluate the same childish behavior very differently. Consider just one common arena for conflict: family mealtime.

Although the mother, in this example, admits that her young children's table manners could use some improving, she has learned to tolerate their noisy chewing and uneaten food left on their plates because she loves them, and as a single parent other matters were more important to address. For the stepfather, however, every meal together has become an excruciating ordeal. Having learned to chew with his mouth closed as a child and to clean his plate, and practiced these behaviors as an adult, he finds their etiquette the very opposite of what he was taught. How important is it to confront this difference? For the stepfather, it seems urgent because the stepchildren's behavior feels so offensive. For the mother, it seems inconsequential because at most her children's manners only feel occasionally annoying. Why is her husband so upset over something that really doesn't bother her? *Because steprelationships amplify the power of negatively perceived family differences.* The stepfather often looks at her children through a different perceptual lens, and both partners need to understand this. Therefore, when he is disturbed by some behavior in the children and she is not, he needs to speak his mind. As husband and wife, they need to talk about what he has found offensive; otherwise unexpressed frustration in him as the stepfather is at risk of turning into resentment at her or the stepchildren.

Very often in remarriage, what the stepfather will consider unusual and objectionable in her children, the mother will treat as normal and acceptable. What is small to her will seem large to him. What is troublesome to him will be tolerable for her. To quarrel about whether he is overreacting to something minor on these occasions, or she is being insensitive to something major, serves no useful purpose. They will always perceive and judge certain aspects of her children somewhat differently—he, often more strictly; she, often more leniently. This is okay. What is *not* okay is breaking the first rule in keeping their relationship healthy: *Never allow differences over the children to become divisive of their marriage.*

How, then, are they supposed to manage these conflicts in parenting? The answer is: *resolve all disagreements over the children without criticizing dimensions of each other that contribute to their differing opinions, but are not likely to change.* What dimensions should they not criticize? There are three:

1. each other's *characteristics* (fixed traits like personal history, temperament, age, and sex);
2. each other's *values* (firm beliefs about right and wrong, or tastes about attractive and unattractive);
3. each other's *habits* (accustomed patterns of behavior like rituals and routines).

For the mother to dismiss his concern about the children's eating by criticizing one of his characteristics ("You've just been a bachelor too long"), for the stepfather to attack her lack of concern as a lack of values ("You didn't bring them up right"), or for each to blame and exaggerate the other's habits ("You always let them get away with everything!" "Well at least I'm not always on their case!") results only in both feeling hurt and becoming defensive. There needs to be another way to manage these differences, and there is.

Three Essential Understandings

First, understand that neither partner is in the marriage to change his or her, or each other's, characteristics, values, or habits. These are largely unalterable dimensions of each other that require respect, acceptance, and tolerance. Pressure to correct them will usually be received for what it is—rejection.

Second, understand that in every marriage there will be some mismatches between one partner's characteristics, values, and habits and those of the other. Individuality dictates that any two people are going to be different from one another. These mismatches will occasionally create *no-fault collisions* between them, clashes of incompatibilities built into the nature of their relationship that neither intended and that will not go away. *Steprelationships tend to increase the number of mismatches in a family, incompatibilities in response to children causing most of the conflicts between parent and stepparent.*

And third, understand that to resolve inevitable conflicts of incompatibility over the children, couples need to translate those differences in characteristics, values, and habits into the specific *wants* they dictate. Then they can resolve these differences in wants by negotiating an agreement each is willing to support.

Return now to resolving the mealtime conflict. Through discussion, the mother has come to appreciate how her husband's history of living quietly alone, the beliefs he was taught about eating in his family, and the etiquette he has practiced over many years all cause him to *want* the children to eat more of their food and eat it more quietly. From their discussion, the stepfather has come to understand how her history in an oppressive marriage, her subsequent belief that children need to have a certain measure of freedom to grow, and her practice of letting them eat as they choose and leave what they choose have all caused her to *want* the children to sit down for a meal and be able to relax.

Armed with these understandings, stepfather and mother can each make some concessions to each other, and compromises with each other, that will allow them to jointly work with the children on some modifications in their mealtime behavior. Perhaps the mother concedes that because the issue feels so important to her husband, she will agree to address the children about it. Perhaps they both agree to a compromise such that talking with the children about table manners will be in the form of a request, not in the form of an order to change their conduct or else. The stepfather gets less than he ideally wanted and the mother gives more than she ideally wanted, but both succeed in constructing a set of conditions their marriage can live with. They may even have added the creative alternative of scheduling separate dinners a few times a week, when they can eat alone without the company of children. Notice that each other's characteristics, values, and habits remain unchallenged and unchanged. (For a fuller discussion of conflict resolution options, see Keys 32–35.)

In working toward agreements over incompatibilities, there are several helpful points to keep in mind:

- Stepchildren should usually not be blamed for causing parental divisiveness between the mother and the stepfather. How these two adults manage their differences on behalf of the children is the parents' responsibility, not the children's fault.
- Neither partner should usually go along with an agreement to resolve a difference simply to appease the other or to avoid discomfort from conflict. What either partner gives into out of fear or fatigue, he or she is likely to regret in anger later.

- With every difference over the children that arises, an opportunity for additional intimacy between the stepfather and the mother is created if they can use the discussion to become better known by each other, and if they can construct another mutually acceptable agreement to bind their relationship closer together. After all, part of the richness of remarriage with children is in its complexity. Two adults are not simply vowing to share a life together as partners; they are marrying on an additional level—as parents as well.

In stepfamilies, because diversity has been increased, incompatibilities abound. They are no one's fault. They won't go away. But as long as they are dealt with on the level of specific wants, they can be appreciated, negotiated, and constructively resolved.

12

OPPORTUNITIES FOR ATTACHMENT

EXPLOITING COMPATIBLE DIFFERENCES

If all diversity between the stepfather and the stepchildren was incompatible, then distance and disagreement would be the best their relationship could offer. Fortunately, this is *not* the case. Many differences can be combined to create positive attachments, if the stepfather, as the adult, will take initiative for seeking these complementary differences out. Ease of establishing attachment will usually vary with the age of the child, the younger being more open and adolescent stepchildren being more resistant.

Attaching to Preadolescent Children

Power differences between the stepfather and the stepchildren can be exploited to mutual advantage. As a mature man with more education, skill, and understanding than a young boy or girl, he can place that competence at the service of his stepchildren's ignorance and inexperience. He can do so by assuming roles to which the children are positively responsive. As a *helper,* he can fix broken objects and figure out problems. As a *teacher,* he can assist in studying for tests and doing homework (without doing it for them). As a *coach,* he can be a practice partner or even manage their team. As an *employer,* he can hire them to do work over and above unpaid family chores in order to earn money.

By entering into any of these roles, he represents a positive new resource for the stepchildren whose reliance and appreciation cause him to feel valued. He receives by giving, they give by receiving, and their relationship is strengthened on each occasion this interchange occurs. Such a positive outcome, of course, assumes he remains patient and uncritical when discharging these roles. If not, then the roles will be rejected by the stepchildren reluctant to get hurt, and valuable bridges across compatible differences will be blocked.

Another complementary role for the stepfather is acting as *provider* to his stepchildren, who are in want or need. This is a useful but trickier interchange to manage. The stepfather usually brings more income into the family, which can mean more money for the stepchildren. He wants to be identified and credited with contributing some of their financial support because this is one sign of his commitment to the family and his caring for them. He needs to refrain from so much material giving, however, that they conclude he is trying to buy his way into their affections, or that money is all he is worth.

A further compatibility to positively exploit is the *spectator/performer difference* in the relationship. Whenever the stepchildren are in a school, community, or church event, are competing in athletics, or are simply wanting to show off something created at home, the stepfather can act as the audience, providing attention and approval that they value. *A stepfather increases the potential audience of adult appreciation in the family.* "Watch me!" "I want to show you something!" "See what I've done!" When the stepfather hears these requests, he knows his approval has come to matter.

Reversing roles is also a way for the stepfather to create closeness through differences. He can ask himself: "What do the stepchildren know that I do not?" When he asks them to teach him a computer game, for example, he develops more sophistication than he had before, whereas his stepchildren increase self-esteem from instructing this grown man. He can ask himself: "What do the stepchildren like to play that I have never tried?" When he asks to be included, stepchildren are given the power of responsibility for initiating a new player into their sport.

By expressing curiosity about the stepchildren's world of interests, and sharing his own world of interests with his stepchildren, differences as well as similarities can be used for mutual invitation. They are eager to see what he does at his job, those activities they do not know how to do but would like to see firsthand. He is unfamiliar with their favorite books, and finds that he enjoys reading these stories to them. When commonality is created, companionship occurs and diversity is shown to be a source of richness in their relationship: the stepfather and the stepchildren directly benefit from this exposure to differences between each other.

Attaching to Adolescent Stepchildren

Teenage stepchildren can pose a greater challenge when it comes to exploiting differences to positive effect. By its very nature, adolescence is a process through which teenagers separate from childhood, family, and parents through the assertion of contrasting differences. "I am different from the way I was as a child. I want to be treated differently than I was as a child. I am different from the way you are as my parents. I intend to be different from how you want me to be. And I am interested in different things that are not supposed to interest you." All of a sudden, the adolescent's world has become posted: "Adults keep out. Parents (and stepparents) will be rejected!"

Does this commitment to an intergenerational demarcation barrier mean that the stepfather should not express interest in his teenage stepchildren's world, should not share his own world of interests with them, and should not make initiatives to get to know them across the differences that seem to divide them? The answer is definitely "No." The stepfather is well advised to continue his expressions of curiosity, his invitations for communication, and his offers for involvement.

The strategies for exploiting compatible differences with young children can sometimes work with adolescents. The key is "sometimes," because teenagers may be less eager to share and less receptive to adult relationships than when they were children. Keep in mind that teenagers are at a resistant age (even with their mother, thus often more so with a stepfather) and may dismiss a lot of his advances. *But not always.* Intermittently, they are open to this connection.

By anticipating this resistance to his initiatives, and by not taking the teenagers' rejections of his openings or advances personally, the stepfather keeps himself in readiness for the opportunity for a connection when it unexpectedly arrives. "Can I go with you to the hunting store?" asks the teenage stepson. "You won't believe what happened in Debate today!" confides the teenage stepdaughter. Why did the teenage stepchildren open up at this particular time? There's no way of knowing for sure, but it doesn't matter. The main point is for the stepfather to be ready to share his world in the first case, and in the second case to learn a little more about what is happening in the teenager's life. After this moment has passed, the adolescent becomes distant again—for a while.

Maintaining consistent initiative and readiness to communicate, in spite of the disinterest, moodiness, and unresponsiveness teenage stepchildren often show, is one of the most important skills a stepfather can develop. Call it *hanging in there.* Call it *refusing to be discouraged by rejection.* This positive persistence will be rewarded with a sustained connection built on small interchanges in which compatible differences have been shared over a difficult developmental time.

PART FOUR

DEFINING THE
STEPFATHER ROLE

13

THE MEANING OF "STEP"

PERCEPTIONS OF THE TITLE MAKE A DIFFERENCE

Titles can make a difference in how people are perceived and treated in relationships. Children, for example, may be more reserved around parental friends addressed as "Mr." or "Mrs." than those who are called on a first-name basis and so feel more relaxing to approach. Even these common titles that children are encouraged to use to show respect for their elders can create distance by imposing formality, connoting authority, and demanding deference.

The title "step," as defined in dictionaries, means "related by virtue of remarriage." The term "stepfather" describes the relationship between a woman's new husband and her children from a previous marriage. What impact the title "stepfather" can have depends partly on what meanings children attach to the term. Some connotations can get in the way of the stepfather's early relationship with them. If he is aware of these connotations, however, and if he listens for statements in which they are commonly conveyed, he can respond to positive effect.

In general, the prefix "step" *modifies* traditional family definitions and in the process can initially cause some confusing distinctions. Modified means *to become different*, but different how? A stepfather is not exactly like a biological father. Stepchildren are not exactly like biological children. Part of the challenge of early remarriage is beginning to work these new definitions out. Remarriage with children creates families in which modified and unmodified relationships must coexist. The stepfather and his stepchildren are in a modified relationship, but the husband and his wife and the mother and her children are not. If the stepfather has children from a previous marriage and from this remarriage, does he treat all three sets of children—mine, yours, and ours—exactly the same? (See Questions and Answers, page 184.)

The question in families created by remarriage becomes: *what difference are step differences going to make?* Beginning to address the relationship with their stepfather, stepchildren frequently answer this question by making definitions and coming to conclusions that can create resistance from the outset of their relationship.

- *"Step" means removed and distant.* Not originating from or growing up with this man their mother married, children can feel they have a long way to travel to get as close to him as to their biological father. They may say something like this: "We feel awkward around you because sometimes it feels like you're a stranger." To which the stepfather might reply: "I know what you mean, because sometimes I feel the same around you. We feel closer to your mother than to each other. It will take time to grow closer with each other and reduce feelings of distance between us."

- *"Step" means different.* Living with a man who is different from their father and mother takes children some getting used to and can create some early discomfort. The unknown part of their stepfather can cause some anxiety at first, not always being able to predict how he will respond or understand exactly what he means or wants. Adjusting to his likes and dislikes can cause them to feel angry, in having to change their lives in order to suit him. They may ask something like this: "Just because you're different, why should we have to act different?" To which the stepfather might reply: "Sometimes I feel the same when I have to adjust how I've been living for your sake. It's going to take each of us making some changes for the other to make our relationship work. What seems hard at first, however, will get easier as we figure out how to live together."

- *"Step" means not real.* For children, the problem with calling their mother's new husband "stepfather" is that this title means he is not their biological father, and therefore has no legitimate claim to treat them like he is. They may say to him something like this: "You're not our real father!" To which the stepfather might reply: "No, I'm not. However, *I am your real stepfather,* and part of your mother and I marrying is both of us agreeing that I will sometimes act as the male parent in this family. It is very important for you to remember that when I act in a fathering way, I am not attempting to actually be your father. Only to help parent you as best I can."

- *"Step" means doesn't count.* Because children have been used to thinking about their single mother as the only parent in the home, they may treat their stepfather as if he is invisible, appearing to walk right through him to get to their mother, and acting as if he isn't even there. Looking for her, they may say to him something like this: "Oh, it's only you. Where's Mom?" Interrupting their mother and stepfather, they may speak directly to her, ignoring his presence and even what he has to say. Dismissing him is their way of not dealing with him. To which the stepfather might reply: "I know it's hard to include me in your thinking about our family, just like it's sometimes hard for me to include you in my thinking about my marriage to your mother. However, you and I both need to take each other into account and show each other consideration in our daily lives."

- *"Step" means inferior.* Most children find it natural to compare their stepfather with their father in order to assert their preference and affirm their loyalty. No matter how they like him, the stepfather is usually a step down from their father in the children's eyes—not as good as, not as loving as, and not as much fun to be with. They may say to him something like this: "Our dad is better than you." To which the stepfather might reply: "I am glad you have a dad you feel good about. I don't expect you to love me or value me the same as you do him. What I do expect, however, is that you and I will be able to develop a good working relationship in this family, find things we like about each other, and find ways we can enjoy being together. That is what I want for us."

- *"Step" means in the way.* One difficulty children encounter with a stepfather is the obstacle he poses in gaining access to their mother. Sometimes it feels like he is an intruder who has come between them and her. Now he and she take time for privacy, or he is there when they only want to talk to her, or what he wants or believes changes the decision their mother makes. They may even complain, saying to him something like this: "Why can't we just have Mom to ourselves?" To which the stepfather might reply: "Because now we each have to *share* your mother. Just like you can't always have her to yourself, neither can I. And this can feel frustrating for both of us, and for your mother who sometimes feels there's not enough of her to go around. But there is, just not always as much as each of us we would ideally like to have. So we must make do with having some of her when we're all together, and more of her when we each have time with her alone."

- *"Step" means not entitled to full authority.* With most stepchildren, there will come a time when they (adolescent children usually challenging the hardest) contest a stepfather's right to assert his authority. Establishing authority with stepchildren requires assuming that power, not asking them for it, having the support of their mother, and usually going through a number of symbolic encounters before that authority is grudgingly accepted. Until then, children may say something like this: "You're not our father! You can't tell us what to do!" To which the stepfather might reply: "Yes, I can. I know you don't like having me make demands and set limits, but when your mother and I married, we both agreed I would help share that hard part of the parenting. It is hard on you, but it is also hard on me, because it is hard on our relationship. Hopefully, when a hard time is over, we can find a good way to be with each other again."

In addition to countering some of the negative definitions of "step" that children may apply, the stepfather can assert three positive interpretations of his own.

- *"Step" means in support of.* Having another caring adult in the home helps share the load of parenting, reduces pressure of sole responsibility on the mother, and increases available resources for the children. The stepfather can honestly say to them: "Now there is more help to go around than there was before."
- *"Step" means standing in for.* When a mother remarries, her new husband does replace the children's father not in person, but in role. Being the salient man in the family on whom the stepchildren can rely for guidance, structure, and supervision may sometimes feel like a thankless task. Assuming that he is caring and constructive in how he acts, however, the stepfather is in fact filling an important need. He can truly say to them: "For your benefit, I am going to do my best to stand in the role of father in this family."
- *"Step" means extended.* Just as marriage extends the family through in-law connections, just as grandchildren extend the network of family affiliation across another generation, so steprelationships extend a family, with the stepfather himself and his whole kinship system now

becoming available to children not biologically his own. A world of special relationships open up—to stepgrandparents, stepuncles, stepaunts, and stepcousins. The stepfather can truly declare to his stepchildren: "Although my family and I were not originally related to you, now we are all meaningfully connected."

14

BEGINNING TO FILL THE FAMILY ROLE

TWO VARIABLES TO CONSIDER

There are as many different ways to define the position of stepfather as there are stepfathers to fill the role. Two basic considerations, however, tend to initially shape the particular definition a stepfather chooses: *receptivity of the children* and *willingness of the mother to share parenting responsibility.*

Receptivity of the Children

One of the best entry strategies for defining a new stepfathering role, particularly if the children are preadolescent, is to let them begin to shape that role with their requests. *How they want to treat him shows how they want to be treated by him.* When they come to him for problem solving, that means they want him to act in the role of *helper.* When they come to him for instruction, that means they want him to act in the role of *teacher.* When they come to him for fun, that means they want him to act in the role of *playmate.* When they come to him to fix a hurt, that means they want him to act in the role of *healer.* When they come to him for encouragement, that means they want him to act in the role of *supporter.* When they invite him to watch their games, that means they want him in the role of *spectator.* When they come to him with something private to disclose, that means they want him to act in the role of *confidant*. When they come to him for permission, that means they want him to act in the role of *authority*.

If the stepfather will listen to the requests of him they make, and if he will ask himself what roles those requests are wanting him to fill, he will discover a host of ways to define himself on terms the stepchildren are ready and eager to accept. He is, of course, not obliged to accept them all. For example, he may refer some requests to their mother that he finds unwelcome or uncomfortable. Perhaps he doesn't want to help rehearse lines for the school play. Perhaps he doesn't want to help bake cookies for the class party. The main point, however, is that by starting with a *responsive role definition,* he is building a relationship with stepchildren that partly fits the one with him that they want.

Willingness of the Mother to Share Parenting Responsibility

Certainly it behooves a man, before marrying a woman with children, to get a sense of her single-parenting philosophy and conduct. In general, if there is a lot about how she raises her children that he does not like or cannot tolerate, he is better off not to make the marriage. After all, he is marrying a family, not just an individual. For a stepfather to enter remarriage resolved to change his wife's mothering will only set a tone of criticism that can lead to conflict, causing her to feel rejected by his demands to change. Should she begin making major parenting changes for his sake, the children will likely resent his interference in their world.

Conversely, if a woman with children is contemplating marriage with a man who expresses disapproval of her parenting and espouses beliefs in child rearing with which she strongly disagrees, she is well advised not to marry him. *Assuming the new husband wants to actively father, she and he need to have some common approach to parenting on which they can agree, and a shared willingness for concession and compromise around those areas where they do not.*

At the outset of remarriage, the mother has a serious question to consider: *To what degree does she want her new husband to be involved in the parenting of her children?* After all, even if she has had some child care support from extended family, she has still grown used to being the primary authority and decision maker with her children. Set in the rules and routines she has created, she relies on them to provide stability for her family. With remarriage, how much of this parenting territory is she willing to surrender and share? Suppose when she does let go of some parenting control, her new husband exercises that responsibility in ways she considers unwise or wrong? *Sharing parenting is an act of trust.* Whereas courtship has caused her to trust him as a person, trust in him as a marriage partner and as a parenting partner will need time and experience to become fully established.

The stepfather needs to understand that building trust for his role in the family relates not only to the children, but to his wife as well. She will naturally be concerned that he treat her children "right." If he becomes angry and impatient while getting the children bathed and down to sleep (because he wants some time alone with her), and the children now routinely become upset at bedtime, she may want to reclaim this parental responsibility for herself.

The stepfather needs to be sympathetic to his wife's caution at letting him in on the parenting. She may need to do it slowly, at first turning over nonsensitive parenting chores like taking the children shopping, or sharing light supervision like making sure weekend chores are done, before wanting him to get into more emotionally loaded areas of responsibility. Exercising corrective authority and getting the children down for the night may be activities she chooses to hold on to in the early stages of remarriage.

If, out of her desire to get the new family up and running right away, the mother pushes the stepfather into too much parenting too fast, he may have to be the one to slow the process down. To take more parental responsibility than he wants, to assume more than the stepchildren can initially accept, will not serve the new family well.

Although the following procedure may sound artificial, it is not. It brings conscious decision making and intentionality to early role definition.

Mother and stepfather can *identify* and *list* all the parenting responsibilities that need to be discharged on a regular basis.

- Mother and stepfather can *rank* them from least to most emotionally sensitive to deliver.
- Mother and stepfather can *come to agreement* about which low sensitive responsibilities the stepfather can assume to begin establishing his parenting role.
- Mother and stepfather can look ahead and discuss the next level of responsibilities he might want to share after the first level have become accepted by the children.

Occasionally, a mother will place the stepfather in a bind by complaining that he is not sufficiently involved with her children, yet she is reluctant to let him in and share direct parenting responsibility. Or she may be willing to let him parent, but only on condition of his strict adherence to her agenda and similarity to her style of operation. In this situation, the stepfather needs to tell his wife that she cannot have it both ways, keeping him out and having him involved at the same time.

Furthermore, just because his way of parenting is not exactly the same as hers does not mean his approach is wrong. He is not calling into question the entire parenting style and structure she has created. He is only asking for inclusion and influence to give meaning to his involvement. If they are going to work together as parents, just as he will try to understand and accept parenting differences with her, he expects her to do the same with him. *Remarriage with children requires that both partners find a common parenting ground upon which the marriage can securely stand.*

15

DETERMINING THE DEGREE OF PARENTAL INVOLVEMENT

FLEXIBILITY OF CHOICE

In simplest terms, the stepfather has three degrees of parenting involvement from which to choose: *co-parent, consulting parent,* or *nonparent.* All three can work well, but each has its own set of advantages and disadvantages attached.

- The stepfather as *co-parent* says to his wife: "In our marriage, I want to assume full standing with you as parent with your children." The *advantage* of this definition is that it maximizes parental involvement for the stepfather with his wife and her children. This means that the husband and the wife agree to spend a lot of time talking together about the children and commit to getting to know each other as parents as well as partners, thereby increasing intimacy between them. It means coordinating their efforts, cooperating on the children's support, and compromising or conceding when parental differences arise. The *disadvantage* of this role definition is that parenting discussions and attention to the children will consume a lot of energy and time, often at the expense of their romantic partnership in marriage. In addition, for the stepfather to assume full power of parent, the mother must be willing to share that power and surrender some control. In the process, they will have parenting conflicts to confront and resolve, and both must expect significant resistance to the stepfather's authority if the children are adolescent. Investing himself fully as a parent when the stepchildren are young lays the groundwork for the stepfather's later relationship with them when they become adults.

- The stepfather as *consulting parent* says to his wife: "I do not want to be on equal parenting footing with you, joining in the daily supervision and direction of the children, but I do want to be able to discuss the children's management and care with you when I have concerns." The *advantage* of this definition is that he gets to have input without having to put in active involvement, whereas his wife gets the benefit of his thinking, still retaining most of the final say in the parenting. They do communicate about the children and he does have social contact with them, but his influence on them is mostly indirect, and with her consent. Direct confrontations between stepfather and children are reduced, because he does not actively set a lot of limits or make a lot of demands. The *disadvantage* of this definition is that she may find his commentary hard to take when he declines backing it up with active support, and he may find it frustrating when she refuses to implement what he believes is a good suggestion. Partly in and partly out of the parenting picture, the stepfather as consulting parent can present a confusing picture to children who don't always know where he stands because he doesn't tell them, preferring to confide his concerns to their mother instead. Because his parental influence may be partly masked to the children, he may sacrifice some parental respect because his lack of direct involvement is interpreted by them as indifference.

- The stepfather as *nonparent* says to his wife: "I married you just to have our relationship, and want to leave all the parenting to you." The *advantage* of this definition is that the stepfather invests minimal time and energy in the children, living around them with his wife who has total, unobstructed responsibility for their care. When together, the couple focus on the marriage, not on parenting. The children as a topic of common concern rarely intrude on their communication as husband and wife. The *disadvantage* of this definition is that the wife is left to mother alone, the stepfather is deprived of a meaningful relationship with her children, and he is essentially disenfranchised from expressing a parental opinion or taking a parental stand when he sees leadership of his wife or behavior in the children of which he disapproves. Uninvolved in their care, however, he must still agree to make room for them in the marriage so that she can spend adequate time and resources on bringing up her children. Over the long haul of the children's growing up, this third degree of parenting involvement of stepfather (uninvolvement) is a recipe for failure for any meaningful future relationship with the adult stepchildren. He who stays out of their lives when they are children is not likely to be invited back in when they reach adulthood, get married, and bring grandchildren around to see their mother.

Stepfathering from each of these separate three definitions can work. Further, in many remarriages there is flexibility such that at different times different levels of the three are taken. The stepfather moves from one degree of involvement to another based on the energy he has to give. Thus, he operates as a co-parent when he has the most energy to give, as a consulting parent when he has less, and as a nonparent when he needs a break from the action to recuperate.

The only way this flexibility works well, however, is if the mother and the stepfather discuss the shifts, agreeing to tailor his role over time to fit his changing tolerances for active parenting, announcing to the children when he is going to be less available or more involved for some period of time. In a way, this is no different than what their mother does as she shifts her availability and involvement with them throughout the day.

It is important for the couple to remember that the mother's relationship to her children is usually more committed and unconditional than is the stepfather's. His commitment takes time to build, and his condition is the need for some positive return on the parenting he gives. It is far easier for him to get fatigued, frustrated, discouraged, and burned-out on parenting, and when he does, decreasing his degree of involvement with the children for a time can help recover his desire to engage as an active stepfather with them again. *It is harder to actively stepparent than to actively parent.*

16

CLAIMING ONE'S MALE DEFINITION #1

THE STEPFATHER AS FAMILY MAN

To marry a woman with children is to take on three male roles at once—as *family man*, as *husband*, and as *father figure*. Although these roles may feel like they are already fixed by society, the stepfather's past history, and expectations of the new family into which he is marrying, they are not. Within each role, the stepfather has enormous latitude of definition and redefinition. By being fully conscious of this freedom, thinking through what kind of role he wants, he can make those definitions intentional and not obligatory repetitions of what he has learned and tried before. By exercising choice, a new stepfather can create an enormously rewarding opportunity for personal growth, as well as making a powerful contribution to the lives of his wife and her children.

More important, *by discussing what traditional definition he wishes to affirm and what he would like to alter, he opens up a dialogue that not only is supportive of himself, but helps unify and increase intimacy in the early marriage as well.*

The Stepfather as Family Man

In the popular culture, there is much more available information about mothering and parenting in media directed toward women than there is about fathering and parenting in media directed toward men. Even in entertainment that focuses on family life, fathers tend to be relegated to the periphery of family functioning, with mothers playing the central parenting role. If the topic of fathering is a relatively neglected one, considered only marginally relevant, the topic of stepfathering, and the contribution a man can make in this role, is even less discussed. And yet, in the majority of remarriages, it is a mother with primary custody of her children becoming married to a man who will occupy the full-time stepparenting role—the stepfather. *There are more full-time stepfathers than full-time stepmothers.*

In reality, stepfathers can derive and provide far more benefit from their role than they are given to initially appreciate. On the most basic level, they *model* what it means to be a family man. Sometimes contrast with the children's biological father can be profound, as they can't help but notice. "Dad liked to work most nights and weekends, and when he came home, he was too tired to be with us. Not like my stepdad, who holds a regular job, comes home in time for supper, and is fun to be with."

A stepfather, however, doesn't have to represent an improvement to have positive impact. He can simply represent an unfamiliar combination of male characteristics that give the children another definition of family man to look at, learn from, and look up to. Children can profit from the new male definition that he brings, because this gives them more adult male diversity to which they can respond and with which they can identify.

But how is a man defined? This question is worthwhile for the stepfather to ask and answer for himself. Even today in the United States, if you look at same-sex peer groups of early adolescents, you will find most boys still being socialized to gather self-esteem and confidence based on how well they *perform,* and most girls being socialized to gather self-esteem and confidence by how well they *relate*. In the process of acquiring these early male and female definitions, each group also tends to emphasize the importance of traits that contrast with the other's. The boys more often focus on companionship (doing together), for example, whereas the girls more often focus on communication (talking together.)

Boys may learn to value acting independently, being competitive, finding ways to challenge themselves, and being private about feelings. *Doing well* may be the key to feeling good about themselves. Girls may learn to value acting nurturing to each other, collaborating, being supportive, and confiding feelings. *Being liked* may be the key to feeling good about themselves.

Vastly oversimplified, this description is only meant to suggest that early male and female sex role development can be quite dehumanizing in the way each sex is culturally discouraged from acquiring the other's human traits: boys suppressing their "female" side ("Don't be sensitive or show fear or pain,") and girls suppressing their "male" side ("Don't be aggressive or act bold or angry"). Approaching adulthood, young men may be socialized to being tough, acting daring, and making conquest, whereas young women may be socialized to being considerate, acting caring, and making commitments. Falling in love begins to break these early sex role stereotypes down. Entering a male/female romance opens up the opportunity for expanding the self-definition of each in the other sex's direction. The male, for example, may learn to share more feelings and respond more empathetically with the female. The female, for example, may learn to enjoy doing more recreational activities that create companionship with the male.

The implication of this early history for discussions between the new stepfather and his wife is that he may want to use his role in the new family as a chance to develop some traits as a man that were suppressed before—as a boy in the family he grew up in, as a younger man among his male peers, or in previous relationships with women. It is a worthwhile question for the stepfather to ask himself: "Do I want to be a different kind of family man than I have been or than I was originally taught?" If so, how?

Within himself or together with his new wife, he can profitably explore certain questions:

- "What ways of being a man have I disallowed myself that I would like to try?"
- "What ways of being a man have I felt forced to fit and would like to give up?"
- "What ways of being a man would I like to be with you?"
- "What ways of being a man would I like to model for your children?"

17

CLAIMING ONE'S MALE DEFINITION #2

THE STEPFATHER AS HUSBAND

The role of husband is defined by how a stepfather treats his new wife. This conduct is watched closely by her children both to see that she is not mistreated (in which case they may rush to her defense) and to observe a different model of marriage that works more happily than the troubled one divorce may have ended with their dad.

By living around it, children register the nature of their mother's remarriage, taking much of it in unawares, but some through conscious study, extracting learnings for later relationships of their own. "I was fourteen when Mom remarried, so I didn't get that close to my stepfather growing up. But he and my mom are very close, and I like the way they are together. If it comes time for me to marry, I hope I find a man who treats me as well."

A well-functioning relationship between their mother and stepfather not only provides children a working model of marriage, but can help restore children's faith in marriage itself, faith that was shaken by the earlier divorce. In this restoration, the stepfather makes a vital contribution as her husband: *His half of the happy marriage to her is also a gift to them.* In addition, he makes three other contributions as a husband: *supporter of the wife's role as mother, keeper of the family priorities,* and *wiser husband.*

Supporter of the Wife's Role as Mother

As a single parent, his wife had no adult partner in the home with whom to share the joys and tribulations of child rearing. She parented alone, and many times felt lonely as a parent. So when she remarries, it is not just adult companionship for which she longs, but for partnership in parenting as well. By the addition of his stepparenting interest and involvement (her new husband listening to her concerns and deliberations, and sharing his own) the base of parental understanding, decision making, and responsibility becomes broader and deeper. Now she has someone to talk to and back her up, and his additional income helps ease her burden of being sole provider.

This amount of monetary contribution needs to be openly discussed (see Questions and Answers, page 184.) He probably should not contribute more financially than he can emotionally afford, or else when the literal and symbolic investment of his resources feel like they are yielding him a poor return ("I help support her kids, but what are they giving back to me?"), resentment may be directed at the marriage.

Keeper of the Family Priorities

If he was not a parent in his previous marriage, the stepfather enters the new one with his wife free of a previous commitment, which she is not—to her children. She and they are bound together by a history he does not share, to which he will always be an outsider. They have a previous claim and future call on her as their mother; she has a previous obligation to care for them until they are grown and will care about them when they are gone. In defining his role as her husband, the stepfather has to accept these realities.

It is natural that she is going to be more focused on *the well-being of the children* than he is. It is also natural, however, that he is going to be more focused on *the well-being of the marriage* than she is. These are two of the three priorities upon which healthy family functioning depends. The third is *the well-being of each marriage partner* themselves. In the long-term interests of the family, the order of priorities is *first,* each partner takes care of his or her own individual well-being; *second,* they both take care of the well-being of the marriage; and *third,* they minister to the well-being of the children. *One role a stepfather can take as a husband is helping keep these priorities in order: 1) personhood, 2) partnerhood, and 3) parenthood.*

Family security and stability flow from the top down, not from the bottom up. A great mistake occurs when the wife and her second husband put the children first, self-sacrificing individual and marital well-being in the process. Then the family collapses around the children, who are often blamed by their mother and stepfather for breaking up the marriage with their insatiable demands. No. In this case, the stepfather and the mother have lost sight of the priorities. By maintaining themselves as individuals, by maintaining the marriage, a healthy family structure will be kept in place to maintain the children.

A stepfather can usually accept his wife's preoccupation with the children if he feels assured that in the larger picture of their relationship and their future life together, she has a primary commitment to the marriage. A stepmother can usually accept her husband's preoccupation with the marriage if she feels assured that he is still committed to the welfare of her children.

A Wiser Husband

Very often a stepfather has had a previous marriage, or at least some history of failed relationships in his past. Assuming he owns his share of responsibility in these failures (and if he does not, he is likely to repeat the error of his old ways), he will want to make some changes in his role as a husband in the new marriage. Perhaps in the last relationship or marriage, he was unsympathetic to the demands of his partner's occupation, always working late at his own job, exhausted and uncommunicative when he got home, investing what energy he did have in the children, and generally was not available to her.

Owning these failings, he may want to bring a different definition of husband to his new marriage. What kind of husband? Again, exploratory questions are worth discussing with his wife who has her own needs for a husband different from the one she had.

- How would he, as a husband, like to support his wife in her role as a mother?
- How would he, as a husband, like to support his wife in her job or career?
- How would he, as a husband, like to keep the marital priorities in order?
- How would he like to be a wiser husband and not repeat the mistakes he made before?

18

CLAIMING ONE'S MALE DEFINITION #3

THE STEPFATHER AS FATHER FIGURE

Regardless of his degree of parenting involvement, by marrying a woman with children the stepfather adopts a father figure role that can be distant when he acts as a nonparent or can be close when he acts as a co-parent. In either case, he becomes the male figurehead of the family, standing alongside the female figurehead, their mother. One way to think about choices for defining the father figure role is to consider it as a personal vehicle for three kinds of giving—to his wife, to his stepchildren, and to himself.

Stepfathering as a Gift to His Wife

Because the mother identifies with her children who are biologically and historically part of her, she takes the stepfather's conduct toward them *personally*. How he cares for them is part of how he cares for her. When he demonstrates interest in them, she warms with appreciation for the attention that he shows. Seeing him lead them, help them, play with them, provide for them, and enjoy them reflects his love for her, because were it not for their marriage, he would not be investing himself in them.

This is a linkage of which the stepfather needs to be ever mindful: *How he treats the children will always be experienced by his wife as part of his treatment of her.*

This awareness becomes particularly important when he has something negative about them to communicate to her. If he is critical and rejecting in his approach, she will feel criticized and rejected. If in anger he threatens: "Change them or else!" he will put her on the defensive, implying she must choose between him or them, tearing her apart with conflicting loyalties for those she loves. When he has objections to her children's behavior, he must be diplomatic, specific, and noninflammatory (see Key 24), or harm can be done to their relationship.

One advantage he has in marriage to a woman with children is that they give him an additional way of expressing love to his wife. She knows they are more difficult for him to deal with than for her. She knows he has no history of love or commitment with them. She knows they give her more of a positive return than they give him. She knows it takes effort, tolerance, and restraint for him to hang in there as an active father figure when they resist or simply take him for granted in this often thankless role. For all these reasons, seeing him persistently and patiently stay involved with them is taken as testimony of his love for her.

Likewise, when her children make an effort to get along with him, she feels grateful to them. This dynamic is central to stepfamily functioning: It makes the mother happy when her husband and children get along, and sad when they do not. Loving them all as she does, she wishes they could love each other as much. Although this degree of bonding is not often possible, the stepfather and the children can try to live together well, weathering the hard times with each other by remembering their mutual love for her.

Stepfathering as a Gift to the Stepchildren

Differences between being a stepmother or a stepfather can depend on how each has been socialized, and on the double standard that society may impose upon their respective stepparenting roles. Just as mothers are still often expected to do more of the active parenting than fathers, the same goes for stepfathers when compared with stepmothers. Stepfathers tend to be given social permission to be less involved with stepchildren. Stepmothers are usually expected to take on more parenting responsibility.

Another factor differentiating a stepmother from a stepfather is how each was socialized to their respective sexual roles. Trained to be feminine by focusing a lot of attention on nurturing relationships and developing intimacy, the stepmother is often most concerned with emotionally attaching to stepchildren, and can become vulnerable to hurt when they express resentment or dislike. Trained to be masculine by focusing a lot of attention on performance and problem solving, the stepfather is often less easily hurt by the stepchildren's rebuffs because he views stepparenting more as part of a family job he has agreed to do. Stepmothers tend to wrestle more with issues of rejection and lack of connection, whereas stepfathers deal more with issues of frustration and lack of power. Insufficient appreciation and obedience are complaints commonly heard from them both.

If the mother wants to retain primary responsibility for parenting, and if the biological father has regular visitation contact with the children, what role is left for the stepfather to fill? A significant one: *the at-home father figure who provides a daily interactive presence in the stepchildren's lives.* This role may not be as glamorous as the entertainment weekends they spend with their father. This role may not be as nurturing as that provided by their mother. However, *by being a contextual part of the stepchildren's family lives,* he provides a male influence that shapes their view of marriage, of fathering, of family, and of themselves from the initiatives he takes and the responses that he gives.

Most children of divorced or abandoned parents have much more exposure to their stepfather than to their biological father, because so many more mothers have custodial responsibility. Time is on the stepfather's side, because he is a fixture in their lives, not just an occasional contact. He can use this contextual time by relating to his stepchildren out of *structured* and *unstructured* fathering roles, making time for both because each has a different quality of contribution to make.

- *Structured fathering* occurs when issues must be addressed, decisions made, and tasks completed. In this part of his role, the stepfather is serious, focused, has an agenda, may be scheduled, and wants to work efficiently. Here, production or problem solving needs to be accomplished.
- *Unstructured fathering* occurs when there is no particular parenting business at hand and no pressure to get anything done. In this part of his role, one hopes the stepfather is relaxed, flexible, responsive, spontaneous, and attentive. Here, room is created with stepchildren for emergent and playful interactions to occur.

The impact of the stepfather is made by continuity, by the accumulated daily structured and unstructured ways he weaves himself into the fabric of their lives over time. *He is there more than the father.* And years later, as adults, many stepchildren finally come to fully appreciate the value of this contribution.

Stepfathering as a Gift to the Stepfather Himself

In two ways, stepfathering can give a man the opportunity to create important changes that feel self-fulfilling. The first change is begun by asking the question: "Would I like to behave differently as a father in this new family than how I did in my previous marriage?" He may desire to learn not only from his mistakes as a husband, but from previous shortcomings as a father as well. Maybe he did not take time to enjoy his children. Maybe he has regrets about being too impatient and demanding. Maybe he was so caught up in his own career needs that he neglected those of his children. *Stepfathering is a chance to redefine his role so that he can be the kind of father he would like to have been.* Altering himself as a father figure with stepchildren can also help him redefine with children of his own when they visit.

The second change is begun by asking the question: "Would I like to experience myself differently from the father I had?" This can be a healing question. Although he cannot undo history and claim a father other than the one he was given, he can try to create a different quality of relationship with stepchildren in which he can capture some of what he missed. "My dad and I could never talk. It was him telling or yelling, and me shutting up and being told. I never got to know him, and he sure never got to know me. At least with my stepchildren, we can communicate, although we often disagree. But there's no yelling when we do. I didn't like being yelled at, and I never wanted to yell at my kids. I'm getting the chance to create some of the fathering I always wanted, but never had."

Focal questions to think about and explore with his wife about his father figure role are as follows:

- How does he want to act as father to her children to reflect his caring for her?
- How does he want to maintain both a structured and unstructured fathering presence in her children's lives?
- How does he want to be the kind of father he would love to have been, or different from the one he had?

PART FIVE

SIGNIFICANT OTHERS

19

STEPFATHERING A STEPSON

SEXUAL COMMONALITY AND COMPETITION

A stepson and a stepdaughter can pose contrasting challenges for the stepfather because of the sexual differences involved. Each stepfamily tie can be rewarding and difficult in its own way.

The Rewards

At first glance, having a stepson appears to be the easier of the two relationships. Because of sexual similarity, the stepfather has an experiential frame of reference for what boyhood is about. Further, he and his stepson may share the same male interests. He likes football; his stepson likes football, and they enjoy playing pass and catch and watching and attending games. He likes to tinker with cars, his stepson is mechanically inclined, and they both enjoy restoring the old automobile in the garage. Because it creates the opportunity for bonding between them, the stepfather's wife supports his time with her son because it gives man and boy a way to be together separate from her.

Beyond the common interests that they may enjoy and the male genetics that they share, the stepfather and the stepson may also share generic similarity based upon how they were socialized as men growing up among their male peers. Part of the masculinity each learned may have emphasized outdoor physical activities, adventuring in search of risk, and the enjoyment of competition to direct growth, define identity, support self-esteem, and form the basis of companionship with friends. If some of this commonality holds, there comes to be a sense of fit between them as the stepson identifies with the man, and the stepfather understands the makeup of the boy.

The Difficulties

On the downside, however, are a number of pitfalls to beware.

First, when the stepfather and stepson have very different male definitions (for example, the child may be sensitive, artistic, and inward, whereas the adult may be aggressive, a leader, and outgoing), each way of being can be difficult for the other to accept. Although he would not anticipate that a stepdaughter was necessarily going to be like himself, the stepfather is more susceptible to expectations of similarity when it comes to a stepson. By proceeding on this expectation, however, reacting disappointedly or critically when the boy does not share his interests and aspirations, the stepfather can send a message of rejection to the stepson, all the while feeling rejected himself. He may erroneously conclude: "If he liked me, he would *be* like me." No. There are as many role definitions of what it means to be a man as there are men to fill them. The stepfather is best served by offering what is meaningful to him as a man, and asking to be shown what is of interest to his stepson. If they do not initially share much similarity, they can develop some by reaching out and learning from each other, with the stepfather leading the way.

Second, the stepfather needs to be watchful if they share a common male dedication to competition. In playing games against each other, winning needs not to be at all costs (roughness causing injury) and losing needs not to give rise to grievance (self-recrimination or anger at defeat). Any contest they play needs to be kept in perspective, seen as a vehicle for companionship where the means is more important than the end. The criterion for a good game is an affirmative answer to the following question: "As a function of competing against each other, do the stepfather and the stepson have fun during the game and feel closer to each other after it is over?"

Third, the stepfather needs to monitor the relationship with his stepson for symbolic competition at home. If the boy has been treated as "man of the house" for many years since his father left or died, relinquishing this position to an outside man can be hard to do. Understanding the difficult adjustment his stepson faces, the stepfather is careful to avoid playing three games:

- Who is the better man?
- Who is the dominant male?
- Who is the mother's primary partner?

To contest any of these questions only affirms the stepson in these roles. More important, if the stepfather actively engages with these conflicts, determined to put the young pretender down, he is at risk of carrying conflict beyond the point of safety into abuse, because the stepson's dedication to competition may disallow him permission to back down.

Instead, the stepfather needs to be aware of these symbolic issues that frequently color the relationship with his stepson. He needs to place his faith in the power of patient insistence, gradually establishing his roles of family man, husband, and father figure in the boy's life.

20

STEPFATHERING A STEPDAUGHTER

SEXUAL DISSIMILARITY AND ATTRACTION

For a stepfather, lacking a common sexual identity and sex role history with his stepdaughter can feel like foreign territory, depending on her age. If she is in the first decade of life, he may feel comfortable treating her as a child first and a girl second, playing freely with her as he would a boy that age. If she is an adolescent, however, now physically and socially developing into a young woman, bridging the sexual differences becomes more challenging. Rewarding connections can be harder to forge; managing closeness becomes more complex.

The Rewards

Perhaps the most enduring contribution a stepfather can make to his stepdaughter's present and future life is by providing her a family example of how a woman can expect to be well treated by a man. As she observes his response to her mother and as she interacts directly with him herself, the stepdaughter can learn important principles of caring, consideration, and respect from men.

If she is of a dating age, the relationship with her stepfather can serve as a reference, helping her discriminate appropriate from inappropriate treatment from younger men. For example, seeing that the stepfather does not try to bully her or her mother when there is a disagreement, she may be encouraged to reject attempts at intimidation from a boyfriend who is getting angry to see if he can get his way. Because her stepfather values her opinions and ideas, and does not simply notice her appearance, she may be less inclined to put up with attention from boys who only respond to her physically, and are not interested in what she thinks or has to say.

As the resident father figure in the home, the stepfather can also contribute a measure of protection when she is dating. Whoever takes her out must first come in and meet with him as well as with her mother, with both parents making it clear that they are trusting the young man to treat her well and bring her back safely.

Sometimes support he gives his stepdaughter can feel unrewarding at the time, like when he joins his wife in taking a stand against the daughter's wants for her best interests. "What your mother and I are saying is that at age sixteen you cannot go to a fraternity party with a college guy." At other times, the stepfather's support can feel rewarding, like when he acts in the role of spectator cheering at her curricular or extracurricular events and taking photographs to commemorate her performance. By the *treatment* he gives, by the *protection* he provides, and by the *support* he offers, the stepfather can play an invaluable role in his stepdaughter's daily life. Appreciating the value of these contributions can be the stepfather's greatest reward.

The Difficulties

If the risks of his relationship with a stepson are rooted in the intensity of possible competition between them, *the risks of the stepfather's relationship with his stepdaughter are rooted in the management of his possible sexual attraction to her, and her possible attraction to him.* Already in a sexually charged relationship with his new wife, the stepfather needs to be careful in his conduct and communication with her adolescent daughter, who is budding into sexuality of her own, her body maturing, her appearance becoming more womanly, and her dress becoming more oriented to earning admiration from men.

Living in household proximity to an attractive young woman with whom he has no history of parental responsibility, and in response to whom he may have occasional sexual thoughts or feelings, the stepfather needs to be ever mindful that his position in his wife's family is one of *trust*. His wife trusts him not to act in any sexually inappropriate way with her daughter, for such a transgression would be deeply destructive to them all. His stepdaughter trusts that he will conduct himself respectfully and responsibly toward her, as a father figure should. He must trust himself to be there in a capacity that makes the family stronger and safer, and not act as an agent of harm.

Drawing boundaries is what keeps intimacy safe. It is perfectly permissible for a stepfather, distracted by his stepdaughter's innocent habit of relaxing in her briefs at home, to tell his wife he would be more comfortable if her daughter lounged around the house more fully clothed when not in the privacy of her room. Just as he is careful to remain fully clothed around his stepdaughter, he would like her to maintain that degree of dress around him. Sometimes adolescent girls will go through a period of testing family tolerance for sexual expression and physical exposure at home, and parents (step or biological) need to set appropriate limits.

The watchword for the stepfather's relationship with his stepdaughter is: *Caution—proceed with care.* How the stepfather looks at her, talks with her, and touches her all have to be within the bounds of nonsexual intent on his side. On her side, he lets the stepdaughter take the lead on what constitutes comfortable terms of affection and limits of intimate touch. If she wishes not to be touched at all and only called by her first name (and not by any other terms of endearment), the stepfather needs to respect her wishes. Conversely, if she becomes the sexual aggressor, treating the stepfather flirtatiously to test her own power of sexual attractiveness at home, he may ask the mother to speak to her about curtailing those behaviors. Without accusing the daughter of acting seductively, the mother can simply say something like this: "We love you and we like how you look, but when you act in these ways it causes both your stepfather and me to feel uncomfortable."

A Final Caution

The following needs to be said, not because this event usually occurs, but because it can. Incidence of incest by stepfathers with stepdaughters is far higher than by fathers with biological daughters, probably because in steprelationships there is no parent/child bonding to provide limited protection against sexual aggression across family ties. This reality must be factored in with another: It is not their male peers who perpetrate most of the sexual violence against young women; teenage girls are primarily sexually victimized by older men.

The management of daily intimacy between an older man and a young girl in a stepfamily places the stepfather in a crucial position of responsibility. It is up to him to keep this intimacy safe, so he can make the significant contributions to his stepdaughter's life that he would like, so that she can learn from him what it means to be well treated by a man.

21

RELATING TO IN-LAWS

PROBLEMS OF REPLACEMENT

To some degree, becoming a stepfather may mean becoming *suspect* for a while in the eyes of one's in-laws. Cause for this distrust are three replacement questions the wife's parents commonly consider:

1. To what degree was the stepfather involved in the breakup of the marriage?
2. Will he make their daughter happy and treat their grandchildren well?
3. Will the new marriage last?

Their acceptance of their new son-in-law can depend on their answers to these questions.

Involvement in the Break-Up of the Marriage

If an extramarital affair with the stepfather contributed to their daughter's divorce, the in-laws may feel compromised in immediately embracing a new son-in-law. It can be hard witnessing dislocation being suffered by their grandchildren, and experiencing some degree of disconnection with the grandchildren's father whom they had grown to treat as family. In consequence, they may have feelings of ambivalence to work through before they can welcome the stepfather as their daughter's husband. Although wanting their daughter to be happy, they are pained by the cost and torn by conflicting loyalties to all of those they love. They may even wonder if by accepting the new marriage, they are somehow endorsing the affair or supporting the divorce.

Understanding that he represents a complicated adjustment for in-laws, the stepfather needs to give them time to work out mixed feelings toward him. "Your parents don't seem to like me," he complains to his wife, feeling discouraged after a visit with her family during which they were warm to her and the grandchildren, but comparatively cool to him. "They just have to get used to you as my husband and to us as a family," replies his wife, and she is correct. *Rather than treat their initial formality and distance as rejection, the stepfather is better off treating it as the beginning of a process of acceptance. This process will gradually unfold over a period of years as they get to know him better, come to trust his love for their child and his caring for their grandchildren, and learn to value him for the individual he is.*

Making Their Daughter Happy and Treating the Grandchildren Well

Parents-in-law are usually slower to accept their daughter's second husband than her first because the family adjustment is much more complex. They still have feelings for their former son-in-law, and an ongoing relationship with him as the grandchildren's father. They have yet to determine the newcomer's fit into the family, his compatibility with their daughter, and his dedication to her children.

"I feel like I am being judged," the stepfather tells his wife, and he is correct. At first, he will be evaluated by their perception of how he cares about their daughter and grandchildren, and how those loved ones show and say they care for him. Adolescent stepchildren can be powerful informants. In discomfort with differences between themselves and him, in defense against an outside adult authority moving in, and in disenchantment with their mother's remarriage on principle of loyalty to their father, they may report negative impressions and complaints about the new stepfather to their grandparents.

This bad press does not initially serve him well. Of course, in-laws are going to sympathize with those they love more than someone who is unfamiliar. At first, they come to know him more through the attitudes of beloved others before relying on direct experience of their own. In general, the younger the stepchildren, the more positive reputation they will give their grandparents about the stepfather. Little children are more likely to bond and adolescents are more likely to balk in this new family relationship (see Key 7).

If in-laws themselves have never directly experienced or indirectly been exposed to the psychological realities of steprelationships, they are likely to be ignorant of the predictable tensions and conflicts that characterize stepfamily life. Instead of perceiving these dynamics as part of the *process* of a reconstituted or blended family, they may identify them as *problems* for which they mistakenly hold the stepfather largely responsible: "There were none of these difficulties before he came."

Should the wife receive this kind of response from her parents, she can helpfully try to educate them about how stepfamilies differ from biological families, telling them what she knows and referring them to some of the many good books on the subject (see Suggested Readings, page 199). When in-laws have an adequate understanding about the complexities of steprelationships, their expectations become more realistic, easing the way for the stepfather's acceptance into their family.

To encourage the connection with his in-laws, it helps if the stepfather is patient and understanding with the conflicts they may feel and the complicated adjustment they have to make. It also helps if, despite their initial reserve, he treats them as warmly and forthrightly as he would like to be treated in return. This initiative is not about pleasing or pretense, and not about currying favor or courting approval. *The stepfather's responsibility to his in-laws is to present himself for who and how he is: open to them and to inclusion by them as a man who loves their daughter, committed to the welfare of her children, and honestly making a full-faith effort to fill a very complex family role.*

Showing That the Marriage Will Last

From the previous divorce, in-laws may have doubts about the stability of their daughter's remarriage, and this distrust of the union may cause reluctance to commit to their new son-in-law. How can they be sure he is here to stay if the marriage may not last? They cannot. So they are inclined to hold back, to wait and see. "They didn't even mention our first anniversary," the wife sadly confides to her husband. "Don't they care?" Yes. It's just that they are not yet true believers. Like stepchildren, it takes in-laws time to accept the permanence of the remarriage.

Although *not* a sufficient reason for the stepfather and his wife to have a child in common, this addition often represents to in-laws an investment in the new family that signifies a commitment to its lasting possibilities. The arrival of this child can also speed their acceptance of the new husband, who is now treated by them not only as a stepfather, but as a father as well.

Even with adding another child, however, it is time that is the great persuader—over passing years, in-laws come to trust their daughter's remarriage and to treat their son-in-law as a permanent and valued part of their extended family life.

The stepfather's parents, as in-laws to his wife, have both her and her children to integrate into their lives. The initial challenge can feel overwhelming. They must get used to their son not only as a husband, but as a stepfather as well. If the stepchildren are young, however, they can very often be effective emissaries for the remarriage, melting the stepgrandparents' hearts and opening the way of acceptance in a hurry. If the children are adolescents, being given special attention and treatment by a whole new set of grandparents can bring out the best in the teenagers in response, and can go a long way in building a sense of extended family for everyone. The stepfather can say to his parents something like this: "As you extend the love you have for me to my new wife and her children, you bring us all into your family circle and cause us to want to include you in ours."

22

RELATING TO THE EX-HUSBAND

PROBLEMS OF SECURITY AND EQUITY

A worthy goal for the stepfather's relationship with his wife's ex-husband is to help create a coalition between separate households to mutually support the well-being of children who grow up going back and forth between the two homes. Working together, parents and stepparents can create a powerful family coalition, pooling collective wisdom, solving common problems, and creating flexibility to adapt to the children's changing needs.

To take advantage of this strength, however, the stepfather may have to address and resolve some common tensions built into his relationship with this "other man" who was the husband of his wife, continues to be her original co-parent, and is the natural father of her children. The stepfather has to *feel securely married to his wife* (and not threatened by her relationship with the ex-husband), and *feel that the ex-husband is contributing his fair share* (and not resenting the father for not fathering responsibly enough).

Feeling Securely Married

Being the second husband means that his wife was once committed to a first with whom she has shared previous history and with whom she had children. On both counts, the stepfather can feel threatened. Being an outsider to an earlier intimacy, he may feel jealous of this prior family claim upon his wife unless he feels assured that as her new husband he has her primary loyalty and love, and her desire for a future with him outweighs the value she places on her past with another man. Yet the past is ever present. There is daily interaction with children from the former marriage. There is contact with their father with whom visitation must be regularly arranged and with whom significant information about the children must be shared.

How is this sharing to be done, and how are these arrangements to be made? Not this way: "When he calls you up at night or you call him and the two of you chat for half an hour about the kids, sharing old memories, I feel you are acting as if you are back together, and I'm left out. Then later, when I'm told about arrangements for the kids you both have made without consulting me, I feel like my concerns don't count, and that you want to honor his desires before mine."

How should her communication with the ex-husband be handled? *First, it should be conducted within sufficient limits so that the stepfather feels comfortable about the appropriateness of that interchange. Second, the stepfather should be sufficiently consulted in the parental decision-making process so that he feels adequately involved.* If issues with the ex-husband ever become divisive of their marriage, the mother and the stepfather need to discuss and redraw the boundaries of their relationship with "the other man" so that their marriage feels secure.

Extremely amicable or embittered divorces can both create problems for subsequent remarriages. In extremely *amicable divorces*, the original couple may get on so well after the dissolution of their marriage that the new husband can feel threatened by his wife's ongoing friendship with her former spouse, who may in turn feel threatened by the stepfather replacing him in the family circle. Should the ex-husband's intrusions disturb the remarriage, the new couple may decide for the stepfather to handle primary contact with the ex-husband, thereby maintaining an adequate connection between the two households while reducing frequency of communication between the former partners. Faced with more contact with the stepfather, the ex-husband can be helped to let his old protectiveness or sense of ownership of the old marriage go, and accept appropriate social separation from his ex-wife.

In extremely *embittered divorces,* unreconciled differences can become inflamed every time the wife and the ex-husband try to share information and make decisions. Or, what was a reasonably amicable divorce can become later inflamed if the mother changes child support or visitation demands out of concern for her children's best interests, acting against what her ex-husband wants or thinks is right. In difficult situations like these, where hard feelings still remain after the divorce is over or are aroused subsequent to divorce, it may be easier for the stepfather to broker more of the direct communication with the ex-husband, because he is not historically or emotionally entangled with the man. For some ex-partners, the wounds from an unhappy marriage, driven deeper by a contested settlement, or provoked by post-settlement changes, may require significant time and separation to heal. If willing, the stepfather can act as a buffer between the two households during this difficult period of adjustment.

The Ex-Husband Contributing His Fair Share

Sometimes it may feel to the stepfather that no matter how actively involved the biological father is in his children's lives, he is never really doing enough. "I help support his kids, provide their daily care, put up with their problems, live around their mess, and get blamed when they don't like our rules because they'd rather get angry at me than at their mother. I'm standing in for him during the hard times while he's off with them on visitation having nothing but good times! It's just not fair!" He is correct. There is much about the step-father's lot in remarried life that is not fair.

It is easy for the stepfather, particularly when living through normal tensions with adolescent stepchildren, to occasionally feel resentful of this inequity. He does more than the father, but gets less appreciation. The father does less, but the kids are always grateful. At times like these, the step-parenting burden can cause him to want to tell the stepchildren how he feels about their father. He needs to resist the temptation. To criticize the father to the children will only turn them against the stepfather. Even in those cases where the father is not socially available or financially making a contribution, most children will still rise to their father's defense.

Children must be left alone to evaluate the adequacy of their father's efforts on their behalf. For the stepfather to express anger over this unfairness to a father directly, this declaration could risk straining a relationship in which the stepfather wants to remain cooperative and supportive. Besides, when the stepfather chose to remarry a custodial mother, he knew he would be committing to live with another man's children.

Yet the resentment at this inequity is recurring, so something must be said. But to whom and how? He needs to be able to talk to his wife, who needs to understand that his occasional resentment at this inequity is human, and that talking about it, without attacking her or her children, helps the stepfather come to terms of acceptance with a situation that will sometimes feel unfair.

If the father delays, is delinquent, or defaults on his child support obligation, it is not unreasonable for the stepfather to want his wife to legally pursue her ex-husband for timely payment of what he owes. Otherwise, the stepfather may feel exploited for contributing to the care of children their father is unwilling to support. At this juncture, if the wife makes excuses for her ex-husband ("He's never been responsible that way, and if I push for money, he may stop seeing the kids"), the stepfather may feel she is sanctioning the inequity that is so troubling to him. *When the stepfather is experiencing resentment from the inequity of caring for another man's children, he needs to be able to talk to his wife about these feelings and she needs to be able to listen. When the ex-husband is not living up to his child support commitments, the stepfather needs to be able to talk with his wife about what steps can be taken so that the children's father contributes his fair share. The emotional costs of inequity must be accepted, but the financial costs of inequity can often be changed.* If the stepfather and the mother cannot talk through these tough issues, they should probably consider getting outside counseling help. Otherwise, conflict that is unresolved may estrange their marriage.

PART SIX

STEPFATHER
COMMUNICATION

23

MANAGING INFORMATION NEEDS IN THE STEPFAMILY

SHARING ENOUGH BUT NOT TOO MUCH

The healthy maintenance of a caring relationship requires that people stay adequately connected so they can share meaningful commonality *together,* and stay adequately *separate* so they can keep their sense of individuality intact. With too much togetherness, people can miss space and time for themselves. With too much separation, they can miss contact and time with each other. On either count, they can feel lonely.

It is through the use of communication that couples in marriage or remarriage and members in a family maintain this delicate balance between separation and togetherness, a balance that continually shifts as growth and circumstance keep dictating individual and family change. Thus, the young child communicates a lot to parents and wants a strong sense of togetherness with them. By contrast, the adolescent tends to communicate less and wants more separation.

In stepfamilies, no topic merits more attention than communication, because the mix of new and unfamiliar human differences can create so many obstacles and can cause so much misunderstanding. *The stepfather's ability to grasp the complexity of stepfamily communication, and to work wisely within it, can contribute much to the healthy functioning of this challenging new family.*

Communication is, at best, a tricky business because in human relationships there are four information needs.

Two serve the cause of sufficient togetherness in a relationship:

1. *the need to know*—to be informed;
2. *the need to be known*—to be understood.

Two serve the cause of adequate separation:

1. *the need not to know*—to remain ignorant;
2. *the need not to be known*—to remain private.

At times, contradictory information needs can create conflict between family members. The stepfather and the mother, for example, may have a *need to know* about what is happening in their teenager's life, whereas the teenager has a *need not to be known*, perhaps because he or she doesn't want to get into trouble. Or the mother may have a *need to be known*, wanting to confide to her teenager painful details about the marriage with her ex-husband, whereas the child has a *need not to know*, because that information will emotionally complicate the relationship with the noncustodial father. In the first case, the child may have to tell more of the truth than he or she wants, and have to face some unwanted consequences. In the second case, the mother may have to keep some marital history to herself to spare her child suffering from hearing all the sordid specifics.

Even when these information needs do not conflict, they can still be problematic in remarriage. For example, when the stepfather's information needs in the new family become frustrated, they yield common complaints to his wife indicating that the couple has some talking to do about their communication.

When his need to know is frustrated, the stepfather may be heard to complain:

- "When you don't even tell me what everyone else in the family knows, I feel excluded and left out."
- "When you withhold important information about the kids, my ignorance makes me anxious, I start imagining the worst, and I end up feeling angry at you for the worrying I've done."

When his need to be known is frustrated, the stepfather may be heard to complain:

- "When no one asks for my ideas or opinions, I feel discounted, like what I think doesn't matter."
- "When you or the kids deliberately ignore my needs and sensitivities, I feel rejected, like you don't care."

When his need not to know is frustrated, the stepfather may be heard to complain:

- "When you and I go out to get away, and all you talk about is problems with the kids, I feel like there is no separate attention being paid to our relationship."
- "When you start talking about some good old times with your ex-husband and the kids, I feel like an outsider in the family."

When his need not to be known is frustrated, the stepfather may be heard to complain:

- "When you tell the kids things about me that I wanted only you to know, I feel like my confidence has been betrayed."
- "When we don't have some privacy off-limits to the kids, I feel they are intruding on our marriage."

The occasion of these or comparable complaints is cause for the stepfather to talk with his wife about how he would like communication structured differently to better serve his desire for adequate separation and togetherness. When their communication needs conflict (she wants to tell others about their problems, he doesn't want others to know), this difference must be reconciled through the tools of change, concession, compromise, or seeking a creative alternative.

Understanding his own information needs of others, however, is only part of the family picture. Family members have their own needs of him that must be recognized and understood as well. As he begins to build his relationship with the stepchildren, his wife can often help the stepfather understand some of their communication needs of him. For example:

- About the stepchildren's *need to know*—"If you would tell them when you are feeling tired from work and need a little time alone to recover after getting home, they won't imagine that you don't care or are upset with them."
- About the stepchildren's *need to be known*—"If you would let the children tell you why they like their music instead of just dismissing it as angry noise, they would feel you were making an effort to understand where they are coming from."
- About the stepchildren's *need not to know*—"If you just answered their homework questions without telling them so much they didn't ask, they would be more receptive to your help."
- About the stepchildren's *need not to be known*—"If you could ask fewer personal questions about their friends, the kids would feel freer bringing those friends home."

His wife can also describe some of her needs:

- To be informed (*the need to know*)—"I know you don't like talking about work when you get home, but I would like to know something about what happens at your job each day."

- To be understood (*the need to be known*)—"I need to tell you what it feels like for me to be caught in the middle when you and the kids have a disagreement."
- To be private (*the need not to be known*)—"Some of what I talk about with my women friends, I would like to remain between them and me."
- To be ignorant (*the need not to know*)—"Unless they are getting in the way of our relationship, I would like it if you could keep some of the minor irritations with the kids to yourself."

The most important topic for the stepfather and his wife to communicate about is couple and family communication. On a regular basis, discuss or at least think about:

- Togetherness—"Is everyone feeling adequately informed and understood?"
- Separation—"Is everyone feeling adequately private and ignorant of what they don't want to know?"

24

NOT MAKING HARD SITUATIONS WORSE

USING NONINFLAMMATORY LANGUAGE

Being a full-time stepfather can sometimes be an exercise in frustration. There are inevitable lifestyle differences between himself and the stepchildren that he will find hard to understand, irritating to accommodate, and difficult to accept. To some degree, these children of his wife were socialized according to a set of family norms, traditions, influences, and rules unlike those by which he was raised. To some degree, he may have parented children of his own very differently. In either case, it is his old frame of family reference that he brings to this newly married life.

His wife is bound to parent differently in certain ways, some of which he may disapprove. "I never would have even considered communicating to my parents the way these kids talk to their mother, and I don't see why she takes it! I was taught to do as I was told and not complain about it, but these kids are constantly questioning her decisions and arguing with her reasons. Whatever happened to the motto my parents believed in: 'Children should be seen and not heard'?" No wonder this stepfather undergoes a certain amount of culture shock entering his wife's family system. The different customs take some getting used to. *Steprelationships are naturally abra-*

sive. No matter how good the blend, some lifestyle differences will become a source of disagreement.

Because of this initial unfamiliarity, how the stepfather responds to different styles of conduct he encounters sets the tone and models the example stepchildren will be encouraged to follow as they struggle to get used to his differences from them. How he chooses to communicate is the key. Although he may feel inclined to let frustration dictate what he says, giving in to this understandable impulse can make a hard situation worse. To prevent this mistake, it is helpful to avoid two common components of *inflammatory language: using abstract name-calling* and talking in *extremes.*

Abstract Name-Calling

The more emotionally intense communication grows, the less operational and neutral and the more abstract and evaluative it may become. Thus, upset by the stepchildren's repeated failures to put back his tools and clean up after playing with them, the stepfather complains to his wife that her children are "scatterbrained and inconsiderate"—two *abstract* words that faithfully convey his feelings of frustration, but to which she takes offense. "Don't call my children names just because you don't like how they are acting. It makes me want to defend them, and it gets me angry at you!"

Actually, he wasn't looking for a fight with his wife; he was really wanting her to hear his feelings and help to solve what was for him becoming a problem. Instead of causing her to want to listen and work with him, however, he has for the moment turned her against him. Now, before they can address the problem together, he must first mend fences with her.

Better for the stepfather to have shared his emotions independently, without attaching them to pejoratives aimed at the children: "Right now I am feeling frustrated and angry about how your children are behaving." Having ventilated some of his feelings, he can then get down to *specifics* by describing *what it is that the children are doing and not doing that is causing him to want to label them as scatterbrained and inconsiderate."*

He explains that by the term "scatterbrained," he was referring to their constantly losing track of the hammers and nails outside. By the term "inconsiderate," he was referring to their habit of blocking the driveway with partially completed wooden constructions. The terms he was using were evaluations reflecting his frustration, not descriptions of the children's behavior. His wife, now hearing him first share feelings with which she can empathize and then state specific objections that she can understand, is better able to accept his concerns and work with him to help address the problem.

Being a stepfather requires a lot of maturity, one part of which is the power of restraint. Upset feelings that steprelationships frequently provoke need to be acknowledged, without allowing these feelings to dictate a use of language provocative to others. The advice here is: *When the stepfather is having a problem with some conduct of the stepchildren or parenting custom of his wife, after expressing his feelings, he needs to be able to describe and discuss what he finds offensive in nonevaluative and objective terms.*

Talking in Extremes

Aggravation at repeat offenses can frequently exaggerate perception of the frequency of that behavior. Thus the stepfather, irritated by one stepchild again forgetting to close the front door, complains: "You *always* let the cold air in" (if it's winter), or "You *always* let the cool air out" (if it's summer). Or, irritated by another stepchild leaving the faucet running one more time, the stepfather complains: "You *never* shut the water off!"

The problem with extreme statements—"You always," "You never"—is that they indict the accused as incorrigible, and they are inaccurate. In response, the person may feel hurt and become more intractable in return. The stepchild thinks, for example: "Since my stepfather believes I never do what he asks, I'll make sure I don't!" In this way, extreme negative statements can actually discourage change by arousing deliberate resistance: "I'll show him!"

In truth, "sometimes" is the more accurate description of the children's conduct. Sometimes they do what the stepfather asks, and sometimes they do not.

If he can hold on to this perception of their mixed performance, the stepfather is actually better positioned to get more of the change he wants. By making an effort to recognize and to appreciate the positive exceptions, he may be able to gradually encourage those occasional instances to become the rule. The advice here is: *Maintaining a moderate view of stepchildren's misconduct allows the stepfather to avoid extreme statements and remain better positioned to encourage the positive change he desires.*

When lifestyle differences in steprelationships become a source for disagreements that need to be resolved by one or both parties having to make some change, *noninflammatory communication* becomes essential. By modeling the use of *specific language* to describe problem behaviors, and by doing so in *moderate terms,* the stepfather sets the tone and provides the example of how this discourse over differences is most productively conducted.

25

COURTESY COUNTS

WHY LITTLE THINGS MEAN A LOT

Courtesy is such an old-fashioned notion that even adults can dismiss its small importance, because dealing with the big events and making the big decisions seem to be more significant contributors to the well-being of family life. Compared to coping with major change, conflict, and crisis, of what importance can taking the time to observe little courtesies possibly be? *A lot.*

To understand the power of courtesy in relationships, consider a hypothetical counseling session between a divorced woman with children, and the man she is planning to marry. Asked to alphabetically identify some qualities they both would like to characterize in their married relationship, they begin their list as follows: "Acceptance, Attention, Approval, Appreciation, and Affection." Then the couple is asked: "What *actions* would have to happen so you would know these abstract qualities were present in the marriage?" Their answer: "We would show them in our treatment of each other." And they describe how this demonstration might occur.

- *Acceptance* could be shown *by listening* to each other.
- *Attention* could be shown by *remembering* promises and special occasions.
- *Approval* could be shown *by complimenting* each other's efforts.

- *Appreciation* could be shown by thanking each other for help.
- *Affection* could be shown *by hugging* each other when departing at the beginning of the workday and when meeting after work is done.

Listening, remembering, complimenting, thanking, and hugging are simply a few of the little courtesy behaviors that express sensitivity and signify that important consideration of the other person is being shown. It is through the regular performance of these small acts that larger meanings are conveyed, and that the quality of daily caring in their relationship is affirmed.

Typically, courtesy behaviors are maintained at a high level during courtship, but then decrease in marriage as each partner makes less of an effort to nourish the relationship and begins to take each other more for granted. In remarriages with children, this omission can be costly. For the stepfather and his wife, maintaining a high level of courtesy with each other is critical, because the demands of remarriage with children is so complex and at times can be so abrasive. On such occasions, when incompatible differences, competing wants, and conflicting views are troubling stepfamily life, it is easy for the couple to become preoccupied with the negative, and to become so busy trying to reach a resolution that they forget to keep up their courtesies with each other. Predictably, when they begin to neglect the small acts of consideration, the positive quality of their relationship begins to suffer. Common complaints then testify to what is lost.

- "You *didn't listen* to a word I said!" (*I feel discounted.*)
- "You *didn't remember* what I asked!" (*I feel ignored.*)
- "You *didn't compliment* the way I fixed things up!" (*I feel rejected.*)
- "You *didn't thank* me for all my help!" (*I feel taken for granted.*)
- "You *don't hug* me anymore!" (*I feel unloved.*)

Courtesy communicates caring through small symbolic acts of sensitivity that signify each partner's commitment to be considerate of each other's needs. The quality of family life is the quality of communication, and the greatest daily contributor to the quality of that communication is courtesy. Both the stepfather and his wife need to observe the important courtesy needs each has of the other, and they need to model courtesy behavior with the children, encouraging that show of consideration in return.

Ask stepchildren how they can tell that their stepfather cares about them and they will describe a variety of small acts of courtesy that show how much he cares.

- "He helps me with my homework." (*Support* is signified.)
- "If I am tired and want to sleep in too late to take the bus, he drives me to school." (*Understanding* is signified.)
- "When I have a game or performance, he always comes to watch, even when it means he has to leave work early and go back and finish up late." (*Sacrifice* is signified.)
- "When Mom and I disagree, he doesn't automatically jump in on her side, but waits until we ask for his opinion." (*Fairness* is signified.)
- "When he and I have an argument, he doesn't lose his temper or act mean. He takes however much time we need to work something out." (*Patience* is signified.)

Stepfathers who regularly maintain courtesy in their communication, particularly when problems arise or conflict occurs, make an invaluable, positive contribution to the quality of stepfamily life. Call it grace under pressure: *Little things can mean a lot.*

PART SEVEN

STEPFATHER
AUTHORITY

26

ESTABLISHING STANDING

UNDERSTANDING THE OPPOSITION

Unless he and his wife have agreed that he will only occupy a marital role and will leave all the parenting decisions to her (see Key 15), the stepfather must address the issue of asserting some degree of authority within the family. To do so requires care and forethought, because the stepchildren, no matter how they like and welcome him as a person, will resist him as a stepparent when he begins to tell them what they can and cannot do. Common complaints about their stepfather's authority often include the following objections:

- "We have to do things differently because of him."
- "He makes rules where there weren't any before."
- "When he doesn't like what I've done, he tells Mom and I get into trouble."
- "He's not my real father, but he acts like he can order me around."
- "He's changed the way my mom used to parent."
- "He's stopped some of the fun I used to have with Mom."

In many cases, the stepfather is guilty as charged, and that's all right. His introduction into the family changes some of the old ways the single-parent family has functioned. For him to get some of his needs and wants met, children in the family must adjust. By becoming the primary partner to their mother, he influences her parenting, her children lose some of their old access to her, and they are no longer the sole focus of her care.

With stepchildren of any age, but particularly with stepchildren in adolescence (from about nine or ten years old and above), it is realistic to expect that they will test and contest the stepfather's early efforts to act in charge. They do this to verify through their experience the answer to three questions:

- "Do you mean what you say?"
- "Does Mom back up what you say?"
- "Do we really have to do what you say?"

In answer to the first question, the stepfather remains firm: "Yes, I would like some help doing the dishes." In answer to the second question, the mother weighs in with her support: "Your stepfather asked you to help him; I expect you to do it." In answer to the third question, the stepfather is prepared to take a stubborn stand against resistance the child may offer. If the child goes on strike—"I won't, you can't make me!"—the stepfather just bides his time, because time is on his side: "I know you would rather be doing something else, but before getting to enjoy what you want, you need to help me with what I want."

Early in the remarriage, it is useful for the stepfather to assert authority over small and routine matters, leaving the larger decisions like denying permission and correcting misbehavior to his wife. It is through making these small demands, best stated in the form of requests, and by making them stick, that the stepfather creates symbolic encounters that signify the authority he is empowered by marriage to their mother to exercise over them. Each time they go along with one of his demands, they begin to build a habit pattern of consent to his authority that makes acceptance of his next demand more automatic.

Here are some suggestions for beginning to establish stepfather authority:

- *Start small.* Compliance with little requests at first builds toward a pattern of larger compliance later.
- *Assume the child will obey.* Acting as if your authority is a given will encourage the stepchild to believe the same.
- *Be firm.* Do not ask for what you are not prepared to pursue.
- *Be willing to listen to objections.* After giving the child a chance to have his or her say (thus saving face by demonstrating some resistance), the stepfather can still expect to get his way (because now the child is ready to give some compliance).
- *Be assured of your wife's agreement.* Do not demand what she won't support.
- *Be cool.* Do not empower the child's natural resistance by becoming upset. Acting matter-of-fact is more productive than acting angry.
- *Be resolved.* If at first you encounter resistance, commit to greater power of insistence. Persistence wears the opposition down.
- *Be appreciative.* No matter how long it took to get the stepchild's cooperation, always end the encounter with the courtesy of a thank-you, thereby modeling appreciation in the relationship.

27

POSITIVE AUTHORITY

BEING PERCEIVED AS A SOURCE OF BENEFIT

For many children, the stereotypes of social authority, particularly for male social authority, tend to be negative—an enforcer of rules, for example, and a restrictor of freedom. In fact, the exercise of authority has a positive side, one that the stepfather wants to assume early on in remarriage to demonstrate that his influence on the stepchildren's lives is not all bad, but can be beneficial.

Because the mother's authority in the family is already embedded in the context of her caring and is historically accepted, she can afford to cede some responsibility for positive parental authority to the stepfather to help him get established with her children. Experiencing their stepfather in the role of "good" authority helps stepchildren tolerate him later on when he inevitably must act in the "bad."

How is positive authority exercised? Consider five contributions it can make: through power of *influence,* of *decision making,* of *resource control,* of *knowledge,* and of *evaluation.* Through the use of these powers, the stepfather can enhance his standing in the stepchildren's eyes.

- Positive *influence* includes *acting as their protector, interceding for them* when they cannot negotiate their way, and *opening up opportunity* out in the world with his connections. As a protector, he can speak to the parents of the child who is threatening his stepchild in middle school and put a stop to the bullying. As an intercessor, with his wife he can meet with the high school counselor to help straighten out a class schedule the stepchild was unable to resolve. As an agent of opportunity, he can, through a friend or an acquaintance, help a stepchild get an interview for his or her first summer job.

- Positive *decision making* includes *giving permission, making exceptions* to rules, and *asserting leadership.* As a permission giver, he can be the parent who chooses to let a stepchild stay overnight with a new friend. As an exception maker, he can be the parent who agrees to let usual Saturday chores be done on this Sunday instead. As a leader, he can be the parent who decides to take the family off on a camping vacation when none of them has ever camped before.

- Positive *control of resources* includes *providing money, giving transportation,* and *financially supporting special interests.* As a provider of money, he can be the parent to whom stepchildren go to get their allowance. As a chauffeur, he can be the parent upon whom they depend for rides to practices, games, movies, and the mall. As a financial supporter, he can be the parent who goes with them to buy the equipment that playing a particular sport requires.

- Positive *knowledge* includes *providing help, giving advice,* and *teaching.* As a helper, he can be the parent who gives homework assistance. As an adviser, he can be the parent who offers useful strategies for solving problems with friends. As a teacher, he can be the parent who, having played the sport when he was young, offers to coach stepchildren in how to improve their skills.

- Positive *evaluation* includes *noticing the positive, giving praise* where it is due, and *rewarding good behavior.* As an observer of the positive, he can be the parent who recognizes signs of progress as the stepchild struggles to resolve a problem. As a praise giver, he can be the parent who appreciates the effort made to master a subject independent of the modest outcome achieved. As a celebrator, he can be the parent who takes everyone out to eat in recognition of a stepchild's work or performance well done.

At least in the early stages of remarriage, it is best for him to exercise positive authority and let his wife discharge the negative side when it is necessary. Thus, when supervisory influence is required by cooperating with the teacher to make sure homework is getting done, let the mother be the parent who communicates with the school. When unpopular decision making is required, let the mother be the parent who denies the twelve-year-old permission to attend a rock concert. When refusal to release resources is required, let the mother be the parent who tells the child that money wanted must be earned and not be given. When gathering knowledge the child does not want discovered is required, let the mother be the parent who checks up on the child to verify what really happened. When an unsatisfactory evaluation must be given, let the mother be the parent who declares falling grades to be inadequate and unacceptable.

Stepchildren who early on are given positive cause to value their stepfather's authority tend to tolerate those disciplinary restraints that he more frequently imposes as he takes the final step toward assuming full parental authority.

28

DISCIPLINARY
AUTHORITY

BEING PERCEIVED AS AN AGENT OF RESTRAINT

After the stepfather has begun to take small symbolic stands with the stepchildren and to exercise positive authority, there remains his taking the final step toward full parental authority: being willing to act as a disciplinary force in their lives. By taking this step, he will occasionally place a strain on his relationship with the stepchildren as he keeps them in compliance with family rules and corrects misbehaviors when they occur. To establish this disciplinary influence, he will rely on five restraints upon which most kinds of social authority depend: *asking questions, making demands, setting limits, applying consequences,* and *confronting issues.* Each time he asserts one of these restraints, his stepchildren probably will not like it, or him, at the time.

- *When he asks a question* ("Why are you so late?"), they may feel that their privacy is invaded and be reluctant to tell.
- *When he makes a demand* ("I want you to pick up your clothes now"), they may feel like they are being ordered around and resent being told what to do.
- *When he sets a limit* ("You can't go to a movie on a school night"), they may dislike being forbidden an important freedom and feel frustrated at being denied.

- *When he applies consequences* ("You're going to have to pay me for damages to the car"), they may not like being punished and object to the cost of reparation.
- *When he confronts issues* ("I want to discuss your conduct at the party"), they may feel he is creating an unpleasant encounter and be defensive about discussing what occurred.

There are two provisos for the stepfather assuming full disciplinary authority. First, it must be with the approval and within the tolerances of his wife so she can fully support him. And second, to the degree he can, it is usually worthwhile to soften the delivery of his stands in order to help make them stick.

Assuring His Wife's Approval

The question to discuss with his wife is: How far should he go to get the compliance or correction he is after? If he is ever unsure, better to err on the side of being too cautious than being too excessive, because it is easier to strengthen an insubstantial stand than it is to undo damage from one that is too harsh.

The mother and the stepfather should be unified in the disciplinary code they uphold and the measures taken to keep the child in compliance. If they become divided, not only are they in conflict with each other, but the child will likely try to exploit that division to his or her advantage. Therefore, clarifying the disciplinary tolerances of his wife becomes a means for solidifying her support.

Thus, his wife may say that questioning the children is fine, but she does not want to turn it into a courtroom interrogation. Making demands is fine, but she does not want them accompanied by threats that create anxiety. Setting limits is fine, but she does not want activities taken away that support the children's self-esteem. Applying consequences is fine, but she does not want them to be physically hurtful or so severely restrictive that they leave the children nothing left to lose. Confronting issues is fine, but she does not want discussion to turn into a personal attack.

Whatever her disciplinary boundaries are, he and she need to clarify them. If he thinks she is too lax or too severe, that also can be considered and altered so that the new step-family code reflects not only her traditional parenting beliefs, but some of his as well. Through this kind of compromise, the children's old family system becomes renormalized to some degree, with the ruling values changing to accommodate the stepfather's influence.

Softening Disciplinary Stands

It is possible for the stepfather to manage each of the five restraining disciplinary acts in ways that can soften their impact and increase the likelihood of their acceptance.

- When posing questions, he can preface them by explaining his need to know and describing the concerns that motivate his asking: "I need this information to assure myself of your safety."
- When asserting demands, he can often offer flexibility for choice within the larger requirement he is making: "This is what I want; when and how is open for discussion."
- When setting limits, he can give an explanation of the risks he is trying to moderate or the evidence of responsibility he would need to justify allowing what he is currently forbidding: "No driving with the distraction of friends in the car until you have established a safety record by yourself—go four months with no accidents or traffic violations."
- When applying consequences, he can separate being upset at the violation from deciding reparation for the act: "First I want to tell you how I feel about what you did, and then I want to take time to think about how you can pay for what happened."
- When confronting an issue, he can focus on the specific behaviors of concern and not on whatever attribute or trait in

the stepchild he may believe these behaviors signify: "I want to discuss how you acted and how you are planning to act differently the next time you are in this situation."

Although there is no popular way to enforce discipline in the lives of his stepchildren, the stepfather can choose to conduct himself in a firm but considerate manner on these occasions, paying the cost of short-term dislike in the present, but earning long-term respect over time.

PART EIGHT

INTENSITY OF STEPFAMILY LIFE

29

THE MANAGEMENT OF EMOTIONALITY

FEELINGS AS GOOD INFORMANTS BUT BAD ADVISERS

It can be helpful for the stepfather to understand that stepfamilies in general, not just his in particular, are naturally emotionally abrasive for at least five reasons:

1. There is household intimacy and interdependence between people who are not all connected biologically or by love, who may at times feel distant from each other while obliged to live closely together on a daily basis.
2. There is an increase of individual diversity in the family caused by remarriage, creating unfamiliar differences that can be hard for members to tolerate and to which it is easy for them all to take offense.
3. For children from the single-parent family, there is increased competition for sharing time and attention with their biological parent who is now by remarriage committed to another adult.
4. For the biological parent, there is stress from being caught between the conflicting demands of spouse and children, all of whom he or she loves, but who often

may not like each other, demanding that their side be taken as a sign of parental loyalty or marital love.

5. For the stepparent, there is continual frustration from having stepchildren constantly around to cause distraction and interfere with the conduct of the marriage, making it hard for the couple to get enough uninterrupted time alone.

Because steprelationships can be so abrasive, effectively managing emotionality becomes one key to keeping the peace in stepfamily life, as members learn not to become inflamed when an irritating difference or an unwanted event occurs. For the stepfather, entering a family system in which upset comes so easily, particularly between himself and the stepchildren, maintaining his *emotional sobriety* (using his feelings for helpful outcomes and not misusing them for hurtful ones) sets a powerful example for them to follow. To do this, he needs to understand how *emotions can be good informants, but bad advisers.*

Emotions as Good Informants

One way to think about *human emotionality* is as *an early awareness system* that has three important functions:

- to *alert* people that something significant is going on in their world of experience by arousing their attention;
- to *inform* people about what is going on by directing their focus;
- to *empower* people to do something about what is going on by energizing their response.

Very often a stepfather may suffer a degree of emotional disability around the recognition and expression of feelings because of the sex role socialization he has received as a male. Perhaps he was taught to be *strong* by controlling emotions and to be *silent* by not expressing them. If so, he can be *insensitive* to himself and consequently can sometimes act in damaging ways to others. For example, by ignoring minor irritations with a stepchild in order to be strong, by building them up into major resentments by being silent, and by at last feeling overloaded, he expresses them in a burst of temper, saying things on angry impulse that he has later cause to regret. It would have served him better to have been sensitive to his feelings as informants, to have focused on whatever offense was going on, and to have spoken up and used the energy of that response to have addressed whatever affront occurred at the time.

Although feelings are neither good nor bad, people tend to assign them that distinction based on how the emotion is experienced. Thus "good" emotions may include pride (focusing on accomplishment), love (focusing on devotion), joy (focusing on fulfillment), interest (focusing on attraction), or gratitude (focusing on appreciation). In general, people are happy to experience these and other positive feelings. "Bad" emotions, by contrast, are unhappy to experience, and may include fear (focusing on danger), pain (focusing on injury), grief (focusing on loss), anger (focusing on violation), or frustration (focusing on blockage).

It is the negative emotions, so easy to feel in stepfamily life, that the stepfather wants to particularly heed. When they make him aware of something problematic in his family world, he needs to be able to speak to his wife about the feelings he has, about what they are in reference to, and, then, about how to constructively deal with the situation. For everyone in stepfamilies, keeping emotionally open (being receptive to feelings) works better than emotionally closing down (being in denial about feelings), and declaring what is felt (being communicative) works better than locking feelings up (being inexpressive). *When hard feelings are not talked out, they are more likely to be stored up, to build up, and to be acted out.*

Emotions as Bad Advisers

Directions for acting out, unfortunately, often seem to be associated with the emotions themselves. Consider just some of the bad advice bad feelings can give.

- Discouragement says keep a negative focus (instead of develop a positive one): "There's no way your kids and I will ever get along!"
- Depression says give in to helplessness (instead of keep trying): "Since most of your family doesn't accept me, there's no point in my making an effort anymore."
- Fear says run away (instead of stand and face): "Why should I hang around and be uncomfortable when your ex comes for the kids when I can leave and avoid seeing him instead?"
- Anger says retaliate (instead of work something out): "When I feel hurt by you, I'll hurt you back!"
- Frustration says force the situation (instead of be patient): "I'll do whatever it takes to get your kids to do what I say when I say it!"
- Loneliness says withdraw (instead of reach out): "If you're too busy with your kids to take time with me, then I don't want to spend any time with you."
- Shame says be secret (instead of confide): "I'll never admit to my wife that I feel jealous when she has time alone with her only child."

Because emotions can be good servants as informants, but bad masters as advisers, it is generally helpful for the stepfather:

- to be mindful that he is living in a family system with a heightened potentiality for emotional abrasion;
- to use his feelings to be sensitive to this complex world of experience;
- to keep current with his feelings by talking them out with his wife and his stepchildren, thereby encouraging them to be able to do the same with him,
- and to be wary of the advice emotions sometimes suggest about how to best respond to those bad feelings when they occur.

30

EMOTIONAL
EXPLOSIONS

UNDERSTANDING OVERREACTIONS
WHEN THEY OCCUR

Even with everyone doing their best to maintain emotional sobriety with each other, occasional unpredictable outbursts will inevitably punctuate stepfamily life. Sometimes, something small and apparently trivial will inexplicably provoke an overreaction in one family member or another. Then the person who exploded may feel regretful and perhaps foolish or ashamed for having become unduly upset without adequate cause.

Those exploded at, perhaps feeling bruised, may blame the overreactor for being oversensitive and unreasonable and blowing everything out of proportion. Maybe there is an apology or maybe not. In either case, the incident is often left unexamined, with everyone just wanting to put the painful episode behind them. This is too bad, because *overreactions have so much to teach.*

The *little incidents* that set people off are actually *significant issues* in disguise. Therefore, whenever emotionally disproportionate responses occur in stepfamily life, it is helpful to take the time afterward, when emotions have cooled down, to discover what the intense outburst was really all about. Overreactions mask important concerns that need to be discussed and understood. Four of the more common kinds of overreactions occur as a function of *suppression, similarity, symbolism,* and *surprise.*

Overreactions from Suppression

Sometimes, when stress from daily friction goes unacknowledged and accumulates over time, it takes only one more little incident for someone's tolerance to be exceeded ("the straw that broke the camel's back"), and previously suppressed tensions all seek release through one emotionally exaggerated response: "I can't stand it any more, the way your kids leave their stuff scattered everywhere!"

Overreactions from suppression occur when the people say to themselves: "This is just too much!" The explosion over one more thing gone wrong ventilates frustration stored up from previous offenses. *To begin to understand this kind of overreaction, ask: "What else upsetting has been happening?"* A stepchild may have been going through a protracted hard time with disloyal friends at school, or the mother may have had a run of rude customers or clients ruin her day. Because neither the child nor the adult felt free to be upset at the time, each came home oversensitized, emotionally loaded up, and easily set off by the next small adversity to come by.

To reduce the likelihood of overreactions from suppression, stepfamily members can commit to emotional currency, resolving to talk with some other family member about what is bothering them when they feel upset.

Overreactions from Similarity

When what happens in the present invokes the painful memory of a similar injury in the past, overreactions may occur. Joking with his wife, the stepfather is caught off guard when she gets furious: "Don't be sarcastic with me; I hate it!" Why did his wife get so upset when he was only teasing? The answer may be because, in his ignorance, he made fun of what was not funny to her. His teasing recalls a significant insult from her past. Overreactions from similarity occur when people say to themselves: "This is just like how I was hurt before!" *To begin to understand this kind of overreaction, ask: "What does this remind you of?"* In this case, his wife may explain that her former husband was continually putting her down, treating her like an inferior, and injuring her self-esteem. Or her children may carry into their mother's remarriage memories of being ridiculed by their father, and so be extremely reactive to the slightest criticism from their stepfather: "I hate it when you act like my dad!" In everybody's past, there are historical hurts not entirely healed that become vulnerable to re-injury when similar insults reoccur.

To reduce the likelihood of overreactions from similarity, stepfamily members can inform each other of these vulnerabilities so that everyone can proceed with consideration around each other's areas of historical sensitivity.

Overreactions from Symbolism

Sometimes an event will occur that feels illustrative of a larger painful truth in a person's life, with the hurt received becoming amplified by what it seems to signify. Thus, when stepchildren initially discount his parental authority and proceed to do exactly as they want despite what they were told, the stepfather becomes furious first at them, and then his wife: "This is just typical of how I get treated!"

To begin to understand this kind of overreaction, ask: "What does this incident represent to you?" In this case, the stepchildren's resistance may be emblematic of an issue that has troubled him since growing up the youngest in a large family where everyone refused to take him seriously or abide by his limits: "No one ever respected what I said!" With this painful truth driving his response, no wonder he overreacted. Or stepchildren become furious with their mother when she reserves two hours of private time at home to spend with her new husband. Asked why they are acting so upset, the younger child finally explains: "It feels like we are being rejected all over again!" The issue of rejection is a sensitive one for them because their father has not seen them since the divorce. Now they are easily wounded by any slights that seem to represent this painful theme.

To reduce the likelihood of overreactions from symbolism, stepfamily members can share with each other the "triggers" that tend to set off those thematic hurts that still trouble them.

Overreactions from Surprise

When stepfamily members get so busy that they do not take the time to keep each other adequately informed about what's happening or going to happen, then surprises can cause overreactions to occur. "You did what? We never talked about that!"

Overreactions from surprise occur when false assumptions are made, or when agreed-upon expectations get violated: "What do you mean we won't be by ourselves this weekend!" And the stepfather storms off while his wife wonders why he is so angry. *To begin to understand this kind of overreaction, ask: "What were you expecting?"* In this case, the stepfather may have assumed the regular pattern of biweekly visitation would continue, and his wife just forgot to tell him about the change. Later he explains: "But I was counting on this weekend with you alone!" Broken assumptions not only yield surprise, but can also provoke anger. Not getting what they expected can be equivalent to not getting what people thought was promised, causing them to feel let down and betrayed.

To reduce the likelihood of overreactions from surprise, stepfamily members can take the time to regularly clarify expectations and check out assumptions by communicating about changes that are going to occur.

Overreactions can be revealing *if* people will try to understand the source and substance of what they are about.

Originally people are usually *unaware* of why they got so upset. Reflection and discussion after the fact is what allows overreactions to become informing. The understanding gained by all parties ideally decreases the likelihood of a similar outburst again.

Because the hidden issues in overreactions can be so valuable for everybody in the family to understand, after feelings have cooled down, the stepfather can take the lead in asking four questions. The answers to one or more of these may help explain the "reason" behind the "unreasonable" outburst.

- The suppression question: "What else upsetting has been going on?"
- The similarity question: "What does this incident remind you of?"
- The symbolism question: "What does this event represent to you?"
- The surprise question: "What were you assuming would happen?"

31

USING YOUR HEAD

HOW PERCEPTION CAN MEDIATE EMOTION

Part of the power of emotionality is its immediacy: *Feelings make experience intensely present.* Thus, like everyone, the stepfather can get lost in the moment when strong feelings take over, be they sadness with his wife or disappointment with his stepchildren. What can be helpful for him to remember on these occasions is that *process* (the experience of what is going on right now) can be the enemy of *perspective* (the sense of operating in a larger time frame bounded by what was and what will be).

Caught up in an angry moment, the stepfather can lose perspective, become trapped in the process, and grow discouraged: "I really resent the stepkids; I always have, and I always will." *Strong feelings can beget unrealistic thinking.* Although emotions speak the truth about the present, they can encourage exaggerated evaluations of the past and the future. In fact, in the case of the disenchanted stepfather quoted above, many good times with the stepchildren have been had before and many others will be enjoyed again.

Once this kind of unrealistic thinking takes hold, however, the stepfather/stepchildren relationship is in danger, and getting outside counseling may be useful to help restore perspective that has been lost. Otherwise, when bad feelings become too frequent or protracted, negative stereotypes of each other can become reinforced. Thus, the irritated stepfather enumerates to himself the offensive traits that seem to typify the stepchildren: "They're inconsiderate, spoiled, selfish, rude, messy, irresponsible, and unappreciative of all I do." Similarly motivated, the irritated stepchildren enumerate to themselves the offensive traits that seem to typify the stepfather: "He's mean, moody, bossy, possessive, distant, insensitive, and uncaring of us."

As long as each side remains stuck in these stereotypical negative sets, it will be all but impossible for them to generate any positive feeling toward each other. Why? Because perception has an enormous influence on emotion. According to a well-known psychological idea, the Thomas Principle: "A situation perceived as real, is real in its consequences." Thus, if the stepfather or the stepchild perceives each other as unfriendly or hostile (whether that is truly how either person feels or not), the consequence will be treating the other person according to that negative perception. In turn, this treatment may encourage an unfriendly or hostile response, providing evidence of what was feared, thereby creating a self-fulfilling prophecy based on what may well have been a false assumption in the first place. "See, I was right!"

There is an extremely helpful question a stepfather can ask himself when feeling upset at his wife or stepchildren. That question is: "What am I thinking?" Consider how this connection works. When something unexpected or unwanted occurs in the family, how he chooses to think about it or *perceive it* can make an enormous difference in his experience. For example, how is a stepfather going to respond when a ten-year-old stepchild spills a glass of milk at the supper table?

If the stepfather *thinks* that people spill things only when they are not acting as careful of themselves and as considerate of others as they should be, he may *feel frustrated* and get *angry:* "Why don't you watch what you're doing and stop being so careless? Now you have ruined the meal for everyone! Go to your room!" If, however, he *thinks* children are distractible and accidents will happen, he takes the spill in stride and *feels undisturbed,* reacting *calmly* by declaring: "Please clean it up." In the first instance, two problems have been created—the spill and his punitive response; in the second, only the spill. Given a choice, most other family members sitting around the table would probably prefer the second response to the first.

The difference in these two emotional reactions is the difference in perception. How people think about what happens influences how they feel about what happens. Most important: *Perception is not fixed or genetic, it is chosen.* The beliefs people hold, the meanings they attach to passing events, and the interpretations they give to what they see are all a matter of choice. The judgmental stepfather who is constantly feeling affronted by the stepchildren's behavior can choose to change his mind, deciding to think in more tolerant terms and to become more accepting, thereby sparing himself and others a lot of his angry feelings.

Mental sets have emotional consequences not just for the stepfather but for everyone in the family. For example, his wife may begin remarriage believing it is her job to make everyone in the stepfamily happy, and so feels guilty when they are not. At last, to do herself a mercy, she decides to change her mind by adopting the belief that, after all, each person is primarily responsible for his or her own emotional well-being. Although she will do what she can to make things work well, she cannot do it all. In consequence of living with this less demanding mental set, she stops feeling so bad about herself when others in the family are discontent. *To change her feelings, she changes her mind.*

To fully accept that perception is a matter of individual choice and can mediate emotion requires that people give up a notion to which they may be strongly attached: that other people can control their feelings. "He's driving me crazy!" declares one stepfather about a stepson who persistently resists going to bed on time. In actuality, the stepfather is choosing to drive himself crazy on behalf of the boy's bedtime behavior by telling himself that his stepson should know when it is time for bed and should go down without delay. "She makes me so angry!" complains another stepfather about a stepdaughter's refusal to get promptly off the phone when told to hang it up. In actuality, what is happening is that this stepfather is choosing to blame his stepdaughter for his feelings that were created by telling himself he should be immediately obeyed, and he is not. In each case, attributing causation of his feelings to his stepchild only creates the erroneous belief that the child has power over the man's emotional state, with the stepfather being a helpless victim of this control.

For stepfathers, the best advice for maintaining emotional serenity amid the complexity of stepfamily life is:

- Use your head.
- Remember, perception mediates emotion.
- If you start to feel upset, ask yourself: "What am I thinking?"
- And if you want to feel better, try changing your interpretations or beliefs.

PART NINE

STEPFATHERING AND THE CONDUCT OF CONFLICT

32

THE CHALLENGE OF STEPFAMILY CONFLICT

USING CONFLICT TO BUILD RELATIONSHIPS

When a mother remarries a man with no children, she just acquires a new partner, but when a man with no children remarries a woman with children, he joins an established family. This difference is why the greatest burden of adjustment in this remarriage is on the stepfather. As the outsider, as the new and different adult joining loved ones used to living together, he has to both make a place for himself and fit into how the family has traditionally been run.

This does not mean that mother and children do not have their adjustments getting used to living with him, but he must get used to more. They each have one new person to get to know, whereas he has many. They all have a longer history with each other than he has with any of them. He will have more that is unfamiliar to get used to, more he will not understand, more ways he will have to change, more lifestyle issues he does not like, and more of those issues to contest if he so chooses. Hence, there can be conflict when, for example, his tolerance for the unfamiliar and his limits of adjustment are exceeded and he feels a need to draw the line. To his wife: "You can't let them talk back to you that way!" To his stepchildren: "Leaving your stuff scattered all around the place like you have is not okay!"

Competence in Conflict

There is probably no competence more important for a stepfather to master than understanding the nature and management of conflict, because so many sources of discord are structured into stepfamily life. Conflict occurs *within* a family member when what that person wants is something he or she also opposes, and struggles for resolution. The stepfather feels torn between saying anything to his wife about his latest irritation with her children and wanting, for her sake, to let the matter go. Conflict occurs *between* any two family members when they agree to disagree over a difference between them and contest the outcome. The stepfather and his wife discover that they have very different standards for how children should clean their rooms, and now must work out those differences. Previous chapters have described some common sources of conflict in stepfamilies, such as ambivalence, change, expectation, competition, diversity, communication, authority, and emotional reactivity, for example.

When it comes to stepfamily conflict, there are two points to keep in mind. First, stepfamilies create complaints and offenses that cause conflict for everyone concerned—stepfather, mother, and children alike. And second, most of these complaints and offenses should not be taken personally, because they are simply built into the structure of stepfamily relationships. Put other players in the place of existing family members, and most of the same discontents and conflicts would arise.

Common Sources of Stepfamily Conflict

Although stepfamilies usually think of these conflicts as unique to their family, in fact, most are built into the nature of stepfamily life. A few of the more common complaints and offenses that can lead to conflict are listed here.

The following are common sources of discontent for the *stepfather*:

- Wanting more time with his wife alone when she wants time with everyone together.
- Wanting more rules and order in the home than his stepchildren or wife agree with.
- Feeling of secondary value to those (children and in-laws) who have a primary connection with the biological father.
- Feeling that he is in a losing rivalry with the stepchildren for the mother's devotion.
- Feeling that he is giving too much effort and getting too little in return.
- Feeling constantly exposed to family behaviors that are offensive and hard to tolerate.
- Feeling taken for granted, taken advantage of, and unappreciated.

The following are common sources of discontent for the *children*:

- Receiving unwelcome, new parenting demands from the stepfather.
- Having the stepfather influence and alter their mother's parenting.
- Having less informal and spontaneous access to their mother.
- Feeling jealous of the stepfather's relationship with their mother.
- Feeling forced to live with a strange adult in the family.
- Feeling uncomfortable seeing their mother affectionate with a man who is not their father.
- Having to accept the stepfather's rule-making parental authority.

The following are common sources of discontent for the *mother*:

- Wanting the stepfather to be less critical of her children.
- Not wanting the stepfather to fully share in parenting decisions.
- Not agreeing with the stepfather's values and beliefs about parenting.
- Wanting the children and the stepfather to get along better.
- Frustration with not being able to make everyone happy.
- Feeling caught in the middle of competing demands between the stepfather and the children.
- Feeling unable to cleanly resolve divided loyalties to the children and to the stepfather.

These conflicts don't mean that something is "wrong" with relationships. They do not mean stepfamily members cannot get along. Conflict is *how* they often need to get along by confronting, discussing, and resolving inevitable human differences and disagreements that arise between them.

The First Priority

The first priority in stepfamily conflict is *not* to resolve the issue at disagreement between people; it is to manage the *emotional arousal* that can develop when people feel frustrated, offended, threatened, or angry in their experience during conflict. Because *safety for all concerned is priority number one*, the means in conflict is always more important than the end, and the process is more important than the outcome, because the welfare of the ongoing relationship is at stake.

It is this emotional arousal that can cause people to "think" with their feelings and act on their emotions. When they do, hurtful words can be said and hurtful actions taken, to everyone's regret. "I didn't mean what I said; I was just feeling upset." "I'm sorry for what I did, I just lost my temper." No. There are no excuses for letting emotional arousal cause the conduct of conflict to become unsafe.

The rule for safety is simply this: *In family conflict, whenever members feel at risk of emotional arousal causing them to say or do something they might regret, they need to declare a time-out. Parties need to separate and cool down, and a later time needs to be set when the disagreement can safely resume.* The same time-out rule holds when someone feels uncomfortable around someone else's emotional intensity.

Here are ten common safety violations in conflict that the stepfather can avoid himself, and help others avoid.

- threats
- yelling
- name-calling
- put-downs
- blame
- criticism
- temper
- manipulation
- retaliation
- hitting

A major part of keeping conflict safe is keeping it clear of behaviors that can do harm. The function of healthy conflict in stepfamily life is to build relationships by helping people confront and adjust to inevitable differences and resolve inevitable disagreements so they can get along better. In his role of "new person in the family," the stepfather, by his example, instruction, and interaction, can lead the way.

33

CONFLICT WITH THE SPOUSE

USING CONFLICT TO STRENGTHEN THE MARRIAGE

Intimacy in marriage is created as partners come to more deeply know and be known by each other. When a man becomes a stepfather, he and his wife create the opportunity for a deeper intimacy than if they brought no children into their union, because now they marry not simply as partners, but as parents as well. They get to know each other and work together in dual roles. Now they have to support not just a marriage, but a family. And now they have to integrate daily child care and child-rearing responsibilities into their new relationship.

Now they each have at least twice as much complexity to understand about each other as they would if both were marrying without children. She has to understand the family values and parental role expectations he brings into the marriage, because they will affect how he perceives and responds to her children. He has to understand the family values and parenting practices she implements, because they reflect how she believes her children should be raised. And if both husband and wife bring children into the remarriage, stepfamily complexity is maximized, because now there are established parenting practices on both sides that must be understood, and there are stepsiblings who have to learn to coexist within the same family.

How to Treat Conflict

The challenge is how to combine these values, histories, practices, and new relationships into a reconstituted family that is conducive to the preservation and growth of a loving marriage. To do so, a lot of adjustments must be made, a lot of differences discussed, and a lot of disagreements worked out. In the words of one stepfather, "I really love this woman, but when it comes to raising her kids, we often don't see eye to eye." So how are partners to conduct and resolve all these experiences with conflict? The answer is, *they must treat conflict as an agent of intimacy that will deepen and strengthen their developing marriage.*

To do this, they must commit to treat conflict *not* as a cause for divisiveness that drives them apart, but as a source of richness that allows them to nurture and grow their relationship. They can reach this goal by subscribing to two objectives when in conflict with each other: to *increase understanding* and to *create unity.* By sharing and listening to each other's point of view, understanding of each other is increased, because conflict allows both parties to feel better known. Using compromise and concession to negotiate a parental response that both are committed to support, unity between them is increased through reaching this agreement. Now by coming to know each other a little better and by finding a way to work together, they have strengthened intimacy in the marriage.

Using Conflict to Marry Differences

Consider the example of the mother's eight-year-old son who breaks his promise to have his chore completed by the time they return from going out. (No one told the sitter, so the sitter didn't know.) For the mother, this offense just warrants holding the boy to the agreement to get the job done. But for the stepfather, this is an infraction that deserves more serious attention. As mother and stepfather discuss what to do, value differences they did not suspect suddenly become apparent. She believes that a child's promise should be treated as an agreement that he needs continuing reminders to keep. The stepfather believes that a child should be taught to be as good as his word, and that some form of corrective consequence should follow any time a promise is broken. She thinks conversation and insistence provide response enough; he thinks punishment should be applied to make a meaningful point.

Now what? Having heard each other out, they elect not to change each other's mind by arguing about who is "right," because that will only polarize the relationship by causing them to defend deeply embedded beliefs. Instead, they act to respect each other's values. They translate their respective values into what each *wants* to happen based on those values, and then they negotiate those wants while leaving the value difference uncontested. Their solution: Combine her desire for conversation with his desire for consequence into a firm talking-to about keeping promises, before the boy is set to completing his chore. Now stepfather and mother are on the same parenting page, and feel more together as a result.

What they have done on this occasion is observe a very important priority. How they deal with a child's misbehavior is secondary to the issue of primary importance, which is to reach a joint disciplinary decision that unifies the marriage, taking however long it takes to get this consensus to happen. They need to use every child-raising decision as an opportunity to create mutual understanding and unity that further marries their relationship.

In addition, by doing so they send an important message to the child: When it comes to discipline, they are unified as parents. Conflict over discipline must never be allowed to become divisive between the parents, because that will weaken the marriage and send a mixed message to the child, who will likely try to exploit it to his advantage.

In their joint parenting, it definitely helps if they treat conflict as just two different ways of looking at the same child-raising concern. By doing so, they can commit to two principles of understanding: that two of them are smarter than one of them, and that both of them are committed to being on the same side—of keeping the marriage strong.

34

CONFLICT WITH THE CHILD

USING CONFLICT TO EXPRESS CONCERN

Conflicts between stepfather and child (childhood ending around ages eight to ten) are formative. That is, they teach the child not only what it feels like to contest disagreement with the new man in the family, but also *how* to conduct conflict with the stepfather based on his example and instruction, and the child's experience in the interaction. Conflict creates resemblance, because when in active disagreement, opponents tend to imitate each other's influential behaviors. When a stepfather models communication in conflict such as listening, empathizing, and collaborative problem solving, the child can be drawn toward following his example. This training can really pay off well in the more stormy adolescent years to come (starting around ages nine to thirteen) if both stepfather and teenager have learned to constructively work out their differences with each other from practice during their childhood time together.

Three-Step Model for Conflict with Children

The model for conducting conflict with children that I recommend to new stepfathers is a three-step one designed for the child to feel the man's concern and so feel comfortable, not threatened or insecure, in the process of disagreement. The three steps are as follopws:

1. *Listen.* Hear the child out without interrupting, becoming impatient, or criticizing. The message of concern to give is: "You have something worth saying, and I want to hear it all." Having been given a full hearing may be enough to satisfy the child, or the stepfather may change his mind. "I didn't realize that this was so important to you."

2. *Empathize.* Be sensitive to and accepting of the child's state without demanding justification for those emotions. The message of concern to give is: "I care to know about how you are feeling." Being responded to with this level of concern may be enough to satisfy the child, or sensitivity to the child's depth of feeling may cause the stepfather to change his mind. "I didn't realize that this was so hurtful to you."

3. *Collaborate.* Treat the disagreement as a problem you both share—in the making and in the fixing. The message of concern to give is: "When we have a conflict, that means we are in this disagreement together and will settle it together." Each having some influence on the outcome may be enough to satisfy both child and stepfather. "We talked it out and worked it out—good for us!"

The purpose of conflict with the child is to show your concern for his or her well-being in these three ways—by listening, empathizing, and collaborating. For example, the six-year old, living with his younger sister and single mother, has been used to entering his mother's bedroom any time he wanted, whether the door was open or closed. Now, with the stepfather moving in, he finds this easy access to his mother reduced, and he doesn't like it. "Why can't I come in when the door is closed?" he complains to the stepfather, who wants the right to bedroom privacy with his wife. So the stepfather begins to deal with the conflict.

1. *He listens.* "Help me understand how you see our disagreement," says the stepfather. "I really want to know." The
boy explains how he has been used to going into his mom's
bedroom when he wanted or needed to at any time, and how
it's not fair that now they keep him out. "I see how it would
look unfair to you," agrees the stepfather. "Getting married
with your mom means she and I sometimes want private time
together, and I can understand how this change means time
apart for you."

2. *He empathizes.* "Tell me how this change in rules
causes you to feel. I really care to know." The boy explains
how not getting to see his mother when he wants to makes
him feel lonely and scared. "And a little sad for missing how it
used to be?" asks the stepfather. "Yes," answers the boy. "And
a little angry at me for getting in the way?" asks the stepfather.
"Yes," the boy agrees. "I'm sorry to cause you unhappiness,"
says the stepfather.

3. *He collaborates.* "Tell me what you think should happen for our disagreement to work out right." The boy is clear:
"I want it to be now like it's always been, that I can come in
whenever I want." "Thank you for telling me what you want,"
says the stepfather. "Maybe we can manage this change to
work something out for both of us." Then they begin a limited
negotiation, the stepfather being flexible where he can be and
firm where he must. "If the closed door means you can't come
in, what can be done to make it less painful for you?" "Can I
knock?" asks the boy.

"Would knocking help?" replies the stepfather. "It would
be something I could do," says the boy. They proceed to work
out an arrangement that helps the boy adjust to this change in
household rules.

The man described the resolution to me this way. "We
reached an agreement where we each had something we had
to understand. He had to understand that from after his bed-

time until we got up, we would have that private time alone. We had to understand what his knocking meant. We even came up with a system. One knock meant he just wanted us to know he was there. Two knocks meant there was something he would like, but could do without. And three knocks meant he really needed us for something important. After a few weeks, he rarely ever knocked at all."

35

CONFLICT WITH THE ADOLESCENT

USING CONFLICT TO BRIDGE GROWING DIFFERENCES

A dolescence (usually beginning around ages nine to thirteen) increases family and stepfamily conflict. This is necessarily so. Normal developmental changes make young people more abrasive to live with as they break the boundaries of childhood to create more freedom to grow. Adolescence can be hard on the mother, but because there is no history of familiarity, bonding, and love, the stepfather is often more likely to take offense at the normal developmental changes that typically occur. Consider the three engines for independence that drive adolescent growth (separation, opposition, and differentiation) and the conflicts for the stepfather that these changes can provoke.

In service of SEPARATION the adolescent pulls away from the nuclear family to form a new family of friends. Now the young person becomes less communicative to create more privacy about this separate social world. Now he or she wants less involvement with the family and more with the company of friends. So begins the *conflicts over distance:* "You never talk to us, you never want to spend any time with us, and you never tell us what is going on!"

In service of OPPOSITION, the adolescent pushes against the rules and restraints of parental authority to assert more power of self-determination. Now the young person tests limits to see what can be gotten away with. Now he or she may even decide that the punishment for taking unauthorized freedom is worth the crime. So begin the *conflicts over disagreement:* "You ignore what we want, resist what we ask for, and argue with everything we say!"

In service of DIFFERENTIATION, the adolescent starts experimenting with new interests, images, and relationships in order to try on new identities. Now the young person fits less well into the family. Now he or she is drawn to models and ideals of self-definition that are unfamiliar to the stepfather and mother, hard to understand, and often harder to accept. So begin the *conflicts over differences:* "How can you like that sort of thing, choose to live like this, and want to dress yourself that way?"

More conflict from distance, disagreements, and differences all come with adolescence.

Adolescent Argument

Adolescence brings on more teenage challenge with authority, and this includes with the stepfather, so he needs to be prepared for more conflict in the form of argument to come his way. He also needs to be mindful about how he may have been trained by earlier experience to manage disagreement as a man, because male and female are often socialized to approach conflict quite differently when young.

In same-sex peer groups growing up, young women often derive self-esteem from relating well with each other, and conflict is dealt with as a chance to strengthen the relationship through communication. The purpose of disagreement is to open up discussion, better understand each other, and work a problem out. Conflict is for having a conversation through bridging differences with interest in finding out what the other person thinks. In this approach to conflict, the person on the other side of a disagreement is treated as an informant.

In same-sex peer groups growing up, young men often derive self-esteem from performing well against each other, and conflict is dealt with as a chance to dominate the relationship through competition. The purpose of disagreement is to close discussion down, argue to win, and get one's way. Conflict is for mastering a challenge through discrediting differences with disapproval. In this approach to conflict, the person on the other side of a disagreement is treated as an opponent.

If a stepfather has been socialized to engage in conflict the "male" way, he will be more at risk of getting into power struggles with an adolescent that may only harden the relationship, make it more difficult to get along, and make mutual resolution harder to reach. For this reason, I usually advise stepfathers to follow more of a "female" model in conflict with their adolescent. This means entering conflict

- as an opportunity to communicate, not as a challenge to control;
- with an open mind, not with one's mind made up;
- discussing to understand, not arguing to win;
- treating the adolescent as an informant, not as an opponent;
- bridging differences with interest, not discrediting them with disapproval; and
- wanting to work toward mutual resolution, not just to get one's way.

Conflict with the adolescent is usually more frequent and intense than with a child. At this age, the young person is both more verbally aggressive and adept, and more willing to engage in argument. However, if the stepfather can call on the listening, empathizing, and collaboration skills he used with the child, and bridge differences and disagreements with interest, conflict becomes not a time for opposition so much as an opportunity for communication. He can accomplish this transformation by drawing the adolescent into further communication with such requests as "Can you tell me more?" and "Can you help me better understand?" Valuing what the teenager has to say, getting to know the young person more than he did before, the stepfather allows him or her the satisfaction of having a fair hearing and a full say. And now conflicts have opened up more communication than they had before.

PART TEN

REMAINING MINDFUL
OF THE MARRIAGE

36

WOMAN IN
THE MIDDLE

RELIEVING PRESSURE ON
THE WIFE'S/MOTHER'S ROLE

Sometimes the stepfather, in moments of family frustration, thinks his wife has it easier than he. Committed by love to a husband and a child who are both more committed to her than to each other, she gets twice as much love as they do. Being more used to the children, she is less prone to upset by some of their ways that he may find offensive. Even when she does not like how the children are behaving, she still has her maternal connection on which to rely, whereas the stepfather lacks that base of love to see him through the hard parenting times. Should he and his new wife become antagonized over some issue or even feel estranged for a while, she still has closeness with her child, whereas the stepfather has no one in the family to turn to for love. For all these reasons, he may feel she enters remarriage at an advantage that he lacks.

There is another side to this perception, however, that the stepfather needs to consider. It has implications for what he can do to protect the marriage by relieving certain pressures that are built into her family position.

Woman in the Middle

Sometimes it can feel like a no-win situation for the mother, as she explains to her new husband: "I hate being caught in the middle when you and the kids want something from me at the same time, or you disagree and expect me to decide between you. How am I supposed to satisfy one of you without frustrating or disappointing the other?"

In stepfamilies, the parent (in this case the mother) is often the object of competing demands that come with the territory of remarriage. She also has to hear complaints about the stepfather and the stepchildren that they, in their frustration, confide to her. Loving them all, it hurts to feel divided loyalties pulling her apart. Criticisms of herself can hurt even more. Her children may complain: "You're always taking his side against ours." Her new husband may complain: "You're always putting them before me."

As she cannot split herself in two, she must accept this conflicted part of her family role. Her husband and her children each feel they should have the superior claim upon her. The children argue: "Remember the past. We were your kids long before you married him." Her husband argues: "Remember the future. I'm going to be your partner long after they are gone." Each believes they have a right to a primary commitment from her in return for the claim they make.

Remarriage with children creates conflicts of sharing. How much should the stepchildren have to share their mother with the stepfather? How much should the stepfather have to share his wife with the stepchildren? How much of herself should the mother share with one of them at the expense of sharing with the other? How much of herself should she share with them both at the expense of reserving some time alone? Often it feels like there is not enough of her to go around, and no way to keep everyone satisfied with her at once.

Understanding the complexity of his wife's position, the stepfather can act to reduce her conflicting pressures.

- *He can take her out of the middle* by letting her know that as far as he is concerned, he does not need to have all her love to get enough. He does not need to act possessive of her with the children.
- *He can take her out of the middle* by letting her know that he does not mind sometimes being put second to her concern for the children as long as she keeps him assured that he comes first as her partner in love. He is satisfied that maternal love for them in no way detracts from her commitment of marital love to him.
- *He can take her out of the middle* by creating situations when it is just himself and the stepchildren together, and she is taking precious time to be with friends or just by herself. He creates an independent relationship with her children.
- *He can take her out of the middle* by taking time away himself, so she can have uncontested contact with her children. He does not act jealous or excluded when she is alone with her kids.
- *He can take her out of the middle* by creating times for him and her to get away as a couple, leaving the children in reliable care. He creates safe separations from family when they can be alone.
- *He can take her out of the middle* by creating occasions when the fun is in all of them being together. He can unify with her in shared enjoyment of the family.

The more his wife feels caught in the middle, the more anxiety-provoking her family life becomes. To cope with what increasingly feels like an impossible situation, she may become other-centered to a fault. She may become self-sacrificing to do what everyone is wanting to make them happy. She may strive to make the family work so she can feel okay, when in fact she feels exhausted and frustrated by continual efforts that fail to satisfy everyone all the time.

From this state of self-neglect, resentment eventually grows as she feels increasingly conflicted about a marriage that is tearing her apart with tensions she alone cannot resolve. To avoid this eventuality, the stepfather is well advised to help reduce those pressures arising from her feeling caught in the middle.

37

CONTRACTING

AGREEMENTS THAT HELP KEEP
THE MARRIAGE TOGETHER

Remarriage with children is challenging because it requires both adults to learn how to partner and parent together at the same time. They are not given the luxury of establishing the marriage before they start a family. The disadvantage of so much to learn so soon is how much adjustment a couple has to make. The advantage is an increased opportunity for intimacy from the beginning of their marriage. In stepfamilies, a man and a woman get to know each other and to become known not only in the roles of husband and wife, but in the roles of mother and father as well.

Given this complexity and richness early on, how can couples successfully negotiate the challenges of this adjustment and claim the gifts of intimacy that remarriage has to offer? By following some guidelines, the marriage can be helped to grow together and not be driven apart by the demands of children and the problems of how to parent them.

Helpful Agreements
- *"We will not argue over whose parenting values are right and whose are wrong."* Value differences over the children are not a problem the couple should avoid; they are a reality to be accepted. Because of their separate backgrounds, the couple will inevitably grow up with different beliefs about

how children should behave and be treated, how much responsibility they should assume, and how much freedom they should be given. Arguing values can polarize the relationship. The more they defend their respective positions, the "righter" both tend to feel and the more firmly opposed to the other each becomes. It is better to accept that value differences are not likely to change, translate those values into wants, and then negotiate the wants to create a position both can support. Thus, the stepfather can declare: "Based on my values, this is the amount of responsibility I want the child to take." The mother can declare: "Based on my values, this is the amount of responsibility I want the child to take." And then, leaving the value differences intact and uncriticized, both reach a compromise between their wants, with each giving some to get agreement. Compromising on value differences does not mean that the couple is abandoning or compromising their values, only creating an agreement with which they both can live.

- *"We will not allow differences over the children to become divisive of our marriage."* If the stepfather and the mother ever find themselves so opposed on behalf of a child that their relationship is being damaged, they need to refocus attention on the higher priority of their marriage. Rather than taking sides against each other, they need to get back on the same side with each other. The prioritizing question is: "What can we each say and do that will restore the sense that our *number one* concern is for the well-being of the marriage we love, that our *number two* concern is with creating a family we both believe in and enjoy, and that our *number three* concern is with coming together as parents around the welfare of the children?" If the first two priorities are honored, the interests of the children will be well served.

- *"We will value each other for the different parenting contribution we each bring to stepfamily life."* What the mother has to offer is a history of understanding from *attachment* that secures children in love. She brings the gift of abiding faith. What the stepfather brings is a current understanding from *detachment* that sees children in more objective terms. He brings the gift of outside perspective. The children can benefit from the confluence of both contributions. Bonded to her children through parental love, the mother needs to accept what is often the lesser parenting connection of the stepfather: "I may not always love or even care for your children, but I am constant in caring about what happens to them, and shall stepparent with that commitment always in mind."

- *"We will agree to treat each other sensitively around the needs for tact and acknowledgment."* There is an exchange that is extremely important for the stepfather and the mother to make with each other, particularly when they are going through hard times with the children. The stepfather needs to be very tactful when making negatively evaluative comments about the children to their mother. To some degree she feels identified with her children, and so can become personally defensive if she feels her children are being criticized ("When you attack my kids I feel attacked"). Exercising tact means that the stepfather will avoid abstract name-calling when describing difficulties with the children ("irresponsible" or "lazy"). He will use objective and specific language that describes behaviors ("not being on time" or "not picking belongings up"). He will not blame the mother for what the children are doing or not doing ("If you'd been more strict, they wouldn't be behaving so badly now"). He will send a mixed message when describing his negative concerns that includes recognition that the children have positive characteristics as well ("Even when they aggravate me, I know they are basically trying hard to get along"). On her side, the mother will constantly acknowledge what her children may take for granted or resent—the stepfather's willingness to share space and resources with her family by investing his time, energy, and caring in children not his own. In many cases, it is often only after the grown children have separated from the home that they can begin to value the stepfather's contribution to their lives and to express acknowledgment of their own. Until then, the mother can fill her new husband's need for this positive response that as the natural parent she needs less, because she gets more of the children's love.

• *"We will take time for ourselves to just enjoy our marriage."* Although it is true that adults with stepchildren who cannot remarry as parents are not likely to sustain marriage as partners, it is also true that remarried couples who are constantly preoccupied with parenting shall fail to sustain the loving partnership they married to enjoy. Time together each day, and occasional time together away when children are not discussed, is essential to the well-being of their married life.

38

THE INVISIBLE MAN

HONORING THE STEPFATHER'S CONTRIBUTION

Sometimes stepfathers can feel *invisible*. Consider these scenarios:

- Stepchildren burst into the room where parent and stepparent are having a quiet talk; they interrupt the conversation to ask their mother a question, ignoring the stepfather by acting like he is not even there.
- Tired of supervising her children to pick up after themselves, the mother complains to the stepfather that he leaves all the parenting work to her, therefore ignoring the daily effort of tolerance and restraint it takes for the stepfather just to live around and put up with the children's messy behavior.
- After a school event where his wife's ex-husband is also in attendance, the children rush up to hug their father and greet their mother when the performance is over, but they act totally oblivious to the stepfather's presence.

To be treated as if one is invisible is a painful experience. It goes beyond rejection. The implied message is: "You don't matter enough to be worthy of notice; you don't do enough to be worthy of notice; you aren't cared for enough to be worthy of notice." Although not the recipient of this treatment all the time, most stepfathers experience invisibility on some occasions.

When they do, it hurts because it feels like none of their contributions to the family count.

Just as the stepfather, for the sake of the marriage, does what he can to take his wife out of the "in-the-middle position," so it is also for the sake of the marriage that his wife regularly recognizes what he gives to her as a parent, to the lives of her children, and to the family. She does this by *appreciating* both his active and passive contributions.

Passive Contributions

The stepfather's passive contributions include

- sharing more privacy, personal space, resources, and relationship to his wife with her children than he would ideally like;
- tolerating and putting up with behavior in the children he may not always like;
- restraining some of the objections and complaints he would like to make, but for the sake of family harmony, he does not; and
- setting some self-interest aside to let the interests of the children be served instead.

Active Contributions

The stepfather's active contributions include

- materially and emotionally helping to support his wife's parenting and the well-being of the family;
- doing for the children, providing services, and giving advice that makes a positive difference in their lives;
- investing energy in parental deliberations and decision making; and
- as another adult authority in the family, sometimes taking unpopular disciplinary stands for the children's best interests against what they want.

By expressly appreciating these and other contributions by the stepfather, his wife gives visibility to *his efforts on behalf of her children.* They are more likely to take for granted or ignore the positive he does, particularly during adolescence when they are often inclined to scapegoat and credit him with blame.

Should this negative perception come to rule her teen-ager's attitude and view, the mother herself may have to brave her child's disapproval. She may openly enumer-ate some of those positive contributions by the stepfather from which the adolescent benefits, and on which he or she depends. Such a statement does not attack the child, but it puts the mother on record as affirming the good the step-father brings to their family life.

As for the stepfather himself, it helps to take a long view of his formative role in the children's growing up. What may be invisible to the children when they are still at home fre-quently becomes apparent after they have moved out and become independent. Looking back, they begin to recognize and value what the presence and influence of this man, not their father, has meant. *He helped secure the family; he helped strengthen the parenting; he cared about what happened to them when they may not have cared about him; and by his example, he shaped some of the ways they learned to believe and to behave.*

For much of this contribution, many stepchildren even-tually come to feel grateful. Through the passing of time, the growing maturity of stepchildren, and the perspective both can provide, the invisible man in the family gains more positive visibility at last than he may have been given at first.

QUESTIONS AND ANSWERS

Should we fully disclose to each other the financial situation we bring into the remarriage, and should we come to an initial agreement about how we want financial sharing in the marriage to work?

Yes. Being open about money before marriage makes it much easier to talk about money during marriage. Having a pre-marital understanding about the division, sharing, and inheritance of separate resources can save a lot of difficult decision making later. If there are significant financial inequities between the partners, and if each is pre-committed to different plans for inheritance, then consulting with a family attorney may be wise. A prenuptial agreement may be helpful to set those matters to rest, along with becoming familiar with the laws governing community property in the state where they are to be married.

Some couples resist an early discussion about money because they believe it only creates discomfort and connotes distrust. Better to get comfortable discussing money right away, and better to treat the willingness to do so as a sign of *mature* commitment between two adults who are unafraid to deal with the practical side of marriage making and family management. As for any agreements they make, the couple is still free to modify them in light of changing circumstances over time, like the couple having a child of their own or the stepfather wanting to adopt the stepchildren.

It just makes good practical sense

1. to disclose what income, assets, expenses, and obligations each partner brings into the marriage;

2. to decide which income, assets, expenses, and obligations will be kept separate and which will be shared in common; and

3. to anticipate, in the event of divorce, how these financial matters would be divided out, and in the event of either partner's death, how inheritance of the estate will be managed.

What kinds of issues should I as a stepfather consider when weighing the possibility of adopting my stepchildren?

The decision to adopt his stepchildren is usually an *emotional* and *social* one for the stepfather. It is also one with *financial* and *legal* consequences that should be taken into account as well. To make an informed decision, he needs to be sure that he can affirmatively respond to all four levels of choice.

1. The *emotional* choice is based on love. The stepfather wants to remove the "step" designation between himself and the stepchildren in order to honor the closeness he feels for them and they for him. The specific change has symbolic value. It signifies that the quality of love between them is of a primary family kind. Although adoption will not alter the emotional relationship between the stepfather and his stepchildren, it will honor and recognize this depth of feeling by choosing to increase their commitment to each other. Often it is meaningful to create some special "family marriage" ceremony to observe this special change, including inviting in close friends and family to celebrate the event.

2. The *social* choice usually involves the stepfather's desire to "get a true family," to be "a real father," and to enjoy "true family feeling." He wants to increase his commitment by altering his social role from stepparent to parent,

and he may want to denote this change by having the children share his last name. Obviously, the choice to adopt is not his alone to make. His wife, the stepchildren, if they are old enough to be aware of the choice being considered, and the biological father all need to concur with this decision. If the stepchildren are adopted in infancy, then they need to be told about the adoption when they reach an age to understand: "I chose to adopt you simply because I love you as my own children." For a stepchild not to be told and then later to discover this truth from some other source can arouse strong feelings of distrust: "What other secrets have you been keeping from me?" Older children need to want adoption in order to support it. If their biological father abandoned contact with them or is deceased, having the stepfather choose to commit to them as their father can be very meaningful to them: "Now we have a father after all"; "Now our last name is the same as everyone else's in the family."

3. The *financial* choice may involve wanting to increase the initial economic commitment to them that he made when he first married their mother: "Now I want to help pay for their college, if they choose to go." There may also be an economic price to pay for adoption if, by law, child support is ended, or to secure the biological father's consent.

4. The *legal* choice, in order to be an informed one, requires consultation with a family attorney who can describe the rights and responsibilities that go with adoption in the stepfather's state of residence. For example, should his remarriage fail, the stepfather will assume all the child support responsibilities of a biological father. He can divorce his wife, but not his adopted children.

With her child, our child, and my child living with us, what is a way to treat each of them fairly so they do not think we are playing favorites?

Fairness is a double standard, with children wanting to be treated the same and differently at the same time. Thus, when the youngest child declares that because all three live in the same family, they should be subject to the same set of rules, the stepfather agrees because equal treatment is only fair. But when the oldest of the three objects and declares that being in high school should bring more freedoms than being in middle school or elementary school, the stepfather agrees because honoring age differences is only fair. Because fairness works in contradictory ways, being perceived as being fair by all the children all the time is an unrealistic goal. Differences and similarities in treatment will bring charges of unfairness from time to time: "You always take their side!" "You let them, but never me!"

A better goal for the stepfather and the mother to declare is this: "Although we have a separate history of love with our own child that we do not have with each other's, *you are now all our own children.* We are equally committed to the welfare of each of you, and in service of that commitment we shall sometimes treat you the same and sometimes differently according to your individual circumstances and changing needs."

If this seems unfair to the children at times, so be it. Maybe the best the stepfather and his wife can hope for is to be perceived as equally unfair most of the time.

My wife says to be patient with her teenage kids—that they are only going through adolescence. But how long is adolescence going to last?

For many a stepfather, the passage of one's stepchildren through adolescence can be the most trying time of all. Adolescents test rules and contest authority, become more self-centered and emotionally intense, prefer the company of friends to family, experiment with risk, and often begin to lie and manipulate to get forbidden freedoms they equate with acting more grown up. Although the whole process of transformation from dependent child to socially independent young adult takes around eight to ten years, achieving full economic self-support can often take even longer. The average age for complete financial self-sufficiency in this country now hovers around twenty-eight. Having a developmental framework of adolescence in mind can help the stepfather gauge where his stepchildren are in the prickly process of growing up and where they are heading next.

- *Early adolescence* (about ages nine to thirteen) is when the child begins separating from childhood by becoming more negative to live with, by actively and passively becoming more resistant to adult demands, and by beginning to test limits at home, rules at school, and laws out in the world to see if they will stick.
- *Mid-adolescence* (about ages thirteen to sixteen) is when the child pushes very hard for the social freedom to be with friends, seems most inconsiderate of others, resents family oversight and restraint, experiments with more high-risk behaviors, and engages in more intense conflict with parents to get his or her way.
- *Late adolescence* (about ages sixteen to eighteen) is when the child wants to engage in more adult relational and recreational behaviors, starts to see social independence more realistically, becomes anxious about his or her capacity to handle so much responsibility, becomes more ambivalent about leaving home, and gives parents double messages about wanting to be self-sufficient and still wanting to be taken care of and supported as a dependent.
- *Trial Independence* (about ages eighteen to twenty-three) begins when the child tries living independently in an apartment, working, or at college studying, discovers the chal-

lenges of more responsibility and self-support, makes and breaks a great variety of commitments (lease, credit, job, education, personal promises, and many others), encounters difficulties in consequence, and learns a lot of good lessons from a host of bad mistakes.

By keeping some perspective on the adolescent process, the stepfather may be better able to remain patient when the hard half of parenting begins.

How should my wife and I manage our affection for each other in front of the kids?

It can be hard for children, who have only seen their mother physically affectionate with their father, now finding her overtly loving with another man. "It doesn't just feel strange and uncomfortable to see my mom kissing a stranger, it feels wrong!" This sense of initial violation, usually most intense when adolescent children are coming into their own sexuality, wears off over time as acceptance of parental remarriage grows. During the early stages of remarriage, however, the stepfather and the mother are wise to keep expressions of their love within the comfort limits of the children. If, when they are being demonstrative with each other, the children look away, walk away, complain how the mother and the stepfather are always loving on each other, or otherwise act embarrassed, the adults just need to go slow in their public display of affection with each other. Not to do so can invite resentment and dislike often more directed at the stepfather than at the mother. To create opportunity for the love and affection they want, the adults need to declare when they want to be by themselves, and let the children know they must now knock on the bedroom door, not just barge in at will as they may have done with their single parent. "We will certainly try not to make you uncomfortable with our expressions of love and affection, but in return you must respect our private time to be alone together."

Does it sound crazy that sometimes my wife feels jealous when my daughter visits us for a weekend?

No, it sounds reasonable. A lot of times a stepfather can be insensitive to the possibility that his visiting daughter, who is insecure in their relationship because of occasional contact and perhaps feeling partly rejected by the divorce, is trying to lay claim to the position of primary woman in his life. The daughter does this by "innocently" interfering in the relationship with his new wife, acting as a rival for his affections, competing for his physical attention, and even driving the wife momentarily away. To the degree that the child acts as an enemy to the marriage, the stepmother may indeed feel resentful and react angrily in return, catching the stepfather in a cross fire between caring for his daughter and commitment to his wife. To reduce the likelihood of jealous conflict arising, the stepfather can structure and conduct the visitation in ways that both satisfy his daughter and do not threaten his wife.

- He can have an understanding with his wife that if at any time during the visitation she feels bothered by the interaction between himself and his daughter, she has only to give a prearranged signal ("There is something I need to talk with you about"), and he will stop action and take private time to discuss her concern. This arrangement gives her some sense of control, in affirming that the conduct of the visitation is up to the adults and not the child.
- Prior to the visit, they can plan a schedule for the weekend that includes not only some special time for the father and the daughter, but also special time with the daughter and other members of the family, and with the whole family together. This schedule would also reserve some private time for the father and his wife to be alone so that the stepmother would not feel she had to totally give up "us" for "her."
- If the daughter seems starved for her father's attention, then he may need to increase phone, written, and impromptu

contact between visitations to create more of a presence in his daughter's life, thereby reducing the extreme pressure to connect on the weekends.

- Certainly the stepfather needs to declare to his wife (the step-mother) that his daughter can never be any rival in marital love, because the roles of a husband and a father are different, his commitment to his wife is primary, and the two roles are noncompetitive and distinct as far as he is concerned. To his daughter, he makes clear that he will always be her loving father, that he hopes she can come to like and appreciate her stepmother, and that this marriage is here to stay.

How should we decide to have a child of our own in addition to the stepchildren we already have?

This decision requires a great deal of thought and discussion. Not only does the stepfather and the mother having a child add to the complexity of family functioning, increase demands for sharing resources, and intensify the competition of needs among existing children, but it changes the marriage relationship by equalizing the parental commitment of both partners to the family. If the husband as a stepfather was only of supplemental parenting assistance, now he becomes fully engaged, with rights to influence and responsibilities for care he may not have had in the family before this time. This is one reason why the stepfather may want to have a child: Stepparenting has aroused his desire to biologically parent and to have that further marital connection with his wife.

There is no absolute criterion for adding "our" child to "yours" and "mine," but there are questions that can be thoughtfully addressed before this decision is finally made.

- *Practically,* can the couple afford the additional demand on their space, time, finances, available energy to give, and existing commitments to respective jobs and to other children?

- *Emotionally,* are they both committed to sacrifice further self-interest and some marital interest for the sake of adding this loving responsibility to their lives?
- *Socially,* are they well enough established as an up-and-running stepfamily that they can add another child member without destabilizing the family system they have worked hard to create?
- *Parentally,* how will responsibilities for the new child be shared, how will the new child be integrated with care for the other children, and how will the other children become involved with their new brother or sister?

Through answering these questions, the stepfather and his wife begin to set realistic expectations about what the addition of "our" child may mean. Finally, of course, it is love that makes the decision. Despite whatever complexities they envision, both partners *feel* they want to further enrich and unify the family by the addition of this child.

Is it especially difficult to stepfather an only child?

Yes. At the beginning of remarriage, many only children powerfully resist the stepfather asserting his rightful place as a third person in the family, as another parenting adult, and as a legitimate marriage partner to the parent. To cope with this resistance, it helps to understand some of the family influences that may have shaped the only child's life before the stepfather arrived upon the scene.

Typically, the only child becomes tightly bonded to parents because he or she is the sole recipient of their love and care. Placed at the center of a world that revolves around his or her needs, the child becomes somewhat self-centered in response, feeling entitled to primary attention and consideration in the family. In addition, by being socialized with adults (there being no other siblings), the only child assumes certain adult characteristics and prerogatives, like being verbally and socially precocious, or having an equal say in family discussions and decision making. Typically, within the family, the only child feels empowered to speak up, and is full of himself or herself because self-expression has been encouraged and self-development has been well nurtured by indulgent parents. Because he or she is their first and last child in one, they want to do their best by this son or daughter (who is the only chance for parenting they get) by doing all they can to make the child happy. All the while, the child wants to do all he or she can to please the parents in return. As they are so closely connected, the parents and the child are highly emotionally sensitized to each other's happiness and unhappiness, and approval and disapproval.

Given so much, the only child has a lot to lose when divorce divides the family world in two. Enormous pain is often experienced by the boy or girl, and enormous feelings of responsibility by the parents. They often carry an extra measure of guilt for their decision, and a resolve to make up for the suffering they caused the child if they can. Subsequent to divorce, there is usually a rebonding between the only child and each parent, bringing them yet closer, particularly with the custodial single parent to whom the only child may attach like a social partner.

Into this dynamic enters the stepfather. Making a place for himself in this new family is going to require that the only child relinquish some traditional standing with the mother to make room for her new husband. This will take time, because the only child's first response is usually to hold on to a dominant position he or she is reluctant to relinquish. In this resistant situation, guidelines for the stepfather include

- being patient, as the child's acceptance will take time;
- being firm to show that resistance will not drive the stepfather away;

- taking time alone with the stepchild to build a special relationship; and
- establishing positive authority as outlined in Key 27 of this book.

To what degree should we allow the stepchildren to speak up, and where should we set the limits?

In general, stepfamily systems in which children are encouraged to talk about their feelings, wants, and thoughts tend to be characterized by closer and less volatile relationships than those in which speaking up is treated as talking back. When shutting up becomes the order of the day, getting to know each other is discouraged and frustrations that are suppressed tend to build up and become increasingly at risk of being acted out in unhappy ways. Stepfamilies are so complex, abrasive, and conflicted that members simply must have the tools of *open communication* to adequately manage the difficulties and differences that naturally arise.

What constitutes open communication? The stepparent and the parent need to define the meaning of the term and to set the rules. *Open communication means encouraging full participation in family discussions within limits set by the adults in charge, according to needs for privacy and competing priorities for time.* Open communication does not mean unlimited discussion any more than inviting the children's input guarantees the outcome they desire. To encourage speaking up, the stepparent and the parent assure *safety:* They shall not criticize different points of view and they shall not punish dissent. They shall, however, model and set standards of exchange such that no one communicates in a way that is hurtful or disrespectful to each other. Within these constraints, the adults promise the children this:

- "In response to the expression of your concern, *we will listen*, although we may not always agree."

- "In response to the explanation of your point of view, *we will reflect understanding* of your opinion, although we may not always change our mind."
- "In response to the questions you ask, *we will answer* as best we can, although we may not always give you the replies you want to hear."
- "In response to confronting us on major objections, *we will seriously consider* your complaints, although we may not always do as you would like."
- "In response to your desire to resolve a family difference, *we will work with you* to settle any disputes, although we may not always settle differences in your favor."

Why is there so much conflict in stepfamily marriages?

In remarriages with children, the increase of human differences and the complexity of sharing create a lot of disagreements to work out. To respect stepfamily diversity, differences in characteristics, values, habits, and wants need to be treated as bridges, not barriers, to further understanding. Each conflict over a difference needs to be treated as an opportunity to come to be known and to know each other more deeply as a person, a parent, and a partner, and as a chance to create a marriage relationship that is tolerant of those differences that cannot be changed.

Learning to share common time, space, resources, relationships, goals, and responsibilities is what creating stepfamilies is all about. Across these categories of sharing, how is the couple going to decide how much is to be "ours," to be "yours," and to be "mine"? The answer is: by agreeing to consider redefining sharing whenever either partner voices one or more of the following sharing complaints.

- "This relationship is *all you.* You make all the major decisions, and I don't like it."
- "This relationship is *all me.* I have to make all the major decisions, and I don't like it."

- "This relationship is *all us*. I didn't marry to give up all my individuality. Too much togetherness is driving us apart."
- "There is *no us* in this relationship. You do your thing; I do my thing; we might as well not be married. Too much separateness is estranging us."

A continuing commitment to discussion, negotiation, and compromise allows the couple to alter agreements about sharing according to constantly changing personal needs and external circumstances—the issues from which conflict is made.

GLOSSARY

Adolescence The period between when a young person leaves childhood, around the age of puberty, and finally grows up enough to accept young adult responsibilities eight to ten years later.

Ambivalence A mixed emotional or mental state in which people feel internally conflicted about a person, experience, or event that they simultaneously like and dislike, or look forward to and dread.

Appendage relationships Extended family relationships created as a function of a marriage or remarriage.

Authority A position of responsibility that empowers the parent to keep children in compliance with the rules of the family system.

Child support A monthly contribution of payments that the noncustodial parent, as a function of a divorce decree or established paternity, agrees to pay the custodial parent to help support any children from their marriage.

Diversity All the different ways any two or more individuals can vary among each other.

Divorce The legal dissolution of a marriage.

Emotional sobriety Using feelings to inform awareness, but relying on judgment to control actions.

Expectations Mental sets used to anticipate what is going to happen in the immediate and distant future.

Incest   Sexual intimacy occuring between nonmarried family members.

Initiation   A ritual through which people pass to change their status or membership in a group.

No-fault collisions   Incompatibilities in characteristics, values, habits, or wants that exist in all relationships as a function of human diversity.

Reframe   To create a broader context in which to consider an issue at disagreement.

Resistance   A person's active or passive opposition to a demand with which he or she does not want to comply, or to a change that he or she does not want to accept.

SUGGESTED READINGS

Deal, Ron. *The Smart Stepfamily: Seven Steps to a Healthy Stepfamily.* Ada, MN: Bethany House, 2006.

Pickhardt, Carl. *The Connected Father: Understanding Your Unique Role and Responsibilities During Your Child's Adolescence.* New York: Palgrave Macmillan, 2007.

———. *Stop the Screaming: How to Turn Angry Conflict with Your Child into Positive Communication.* New York: Palgrave Macmillan, 2009.

Wisdom, Susan and Jennifer Green. *Stepcoupling: Creating and Sustaining a Strong Marriage in Today's Blended Family.* New York: Three Rivers Press, 2002.

Ziegahn, Susan J. *7 Steps to Bonding with Your Stepchild.* New York: St. Martin's Griffin, 2001.

INDEX